BFI FILM CLASSICS

. . . .

Rob White
SERIES EDITOR

Edward Buscombe, Colin MacCabe, David Meeker and Markku Salmi
SERIES CONSULTANTS

Launched in 1992, BFI Film Classics is a series of books that introduces, interprets and honours 360 landmark works of world cinema. The series includes a wide range of approaches and critical styles, reflecting the diverse ways we appreciate, analyse and enjoy great films.

A treasury that keeps on delivering ... any film person needs the whole collection.
Independent on Sunday

Magnificently concentrated examples of flowing freeform critical poetry.
Uncut

A formidable body of work collectively generating some fascinating insights into the evolution of cinema.
Times Higher Education Supplement

The definitive film companion essays.
Hotdog

The choice of authors is as judicious, eclectic and original as the choice of titles.
Positif

Estimable.
Boston Globe

Invaluable.
Los Angeles Times

The series is a landmark in the history of film criticism.
Quarterly Review of Film and Video

Well written, impeccably researched and beautifully presented ... as a publishing venture, it is difficult to fault.
Film Ireland

Michael Hamer (far left) and Michael Balcon (in the glasses) on the set of *Kind Hearts and Coronets*

BFI FILM CLASSICS

KIND HEARTS
AND CORONETS

· · · · · · · · · · · · · · · · · ·

Michael Newton

 Publishing

First published in 2003 by the
BRITISH FILM INSTITUTE
21 Stephen Street, London W1T 1LN

The British Film Institute
promotes greater understanding
and appreciation of, and
access to, film and moving image
culture in the UK.

British Library Cataloguing-in-Publication Data
A catalogue record for this book is available from the British Library

ISBN 0–85170–964–8

Series design by
Andrew Barron & Collis Clements Associates

Typeset in Fournier and Franklin Gothic by
D R Bungay Associates, Burghfield, Berks

Printed in Great Britain by Cromwell Press, Trowbridge, Wiltshire

CONTENTS

ACKNOWLEDGMENTS

I would like to thank: Rob White for his skill and patience as an editor; Professor Michael Wood for helping me to get started; the library, archive and publishing staff at the British Film Institute, The British Library and the Museum of London; Professor Philip Horne, for the loan of the videos; Dr Greg Dart and his Post-War British Comedy seminar group (especially Katie Dailey and Helen Taylor); Rebecca Arnold and Marketa Uhlirova; David Trotter, Kasia Boddy and Daniel Karlin for helpful comments made at the UCL Graduate Seminar; Dr Christopher Hamilton for helping out brilliantly (as ever) with the German; Sarah Lusznat, for helping me to look at things; my mother and father for the support that made the difference. This book is dedicated to my favourite actor.

Louis writes his story

'KIND HEARTS AND CORONETS'

....

Though all things foul would wear the brows of grace,
Yet grace must still look so.
  Shakespeare, *Macbeth*[1]

What were the possibilities which thus presented themselves? Firstly,
that of making a film not noticeably similar to any previously made in
the English language. Secondly, that of using this English language,
which I love, in a more varied and, to me, more interesting way than I
had previously had the chance of doing in a film. Thirdly, that of making
a picture which paid no regard whatever to established, although not
practised, moral convention. This last was not from any desire to shock,
but from an impulse to escape the somewhat inflexible and unshaded
characterization which convention tends to enforce in scripts.
  Robert Hamer[2]

From among a crowd of adoring women, a plucky suffragette in a hot-air
balloon sails away into the skies of London. Looking slightly queasy, she
flings handfuls of leaflets over the West End. Suddenly we see a neat
young man at an open window, incongruously clutching a bow and
arrow. Kneeling, cupid-like, he takes aim and lets fly. A voice, the young
man's, tells us what happens next: 'I shot an arrow in the air; She fell to
earth in Berkeley Square.' It is a great moment of British film comedy,
because, of course, nothing here is as it seems: a man in drag plays the
suffragette; the archer's wit is murderous.

Lady Agatha aloft

Here's another scene from the same film. Again our young hero is on the screen, and on the surface he appears a model of good breeding, although perhaps dressed a little too well in a satin dressing gown. Nonchalantly he reclines on a sofa, sipping sherry. Hearing someone at the door, he rises and lets in an attractive young woman, wearing a feathered hat that is likewise somehow too splendid. She has terrible news: last night, their affair was discovered! The young man listens, remaining sardonically placid throughout her revelations. Yet the woman persists. Some scandal may yet be averted, and her husband may allow her a divorce, if she could only tell him that she will be marrying again. Unmoved, the young man tells her: 'Not only do I know you're blackmailing me – an ugly word, but the only appropriate one – but I also know that you're bluffing me!' He met her husband only an hour before, and the fool clearly knew nothing of any affair. In any case, even if she did divorce her husband, they could never marry; for the young man is already engaged to another woman, a well-born widow. The blackmailer seethes, controlling her fury. But the young man merely places a finger on her chin: 'Has it ever occurred to you, Sibella, that we serve each other right, you and I?' Dignified to the last, Sibella coolly replies: 'Would it be asking too much of your manners to escort me to the door?' Silently, he shows her out.

The scene veers towards the cheapest cliché. Tired melodrama drags itself before us, and we fear that we are witnessing yet again a scene we've endured a thousand times before. But the film quickly reassures us. The lovers already know this is just such a scene, and that they are only players.

Love in a cold climate

Moreover the emotions on screen are almost puzzlingly new. Their liaison betrays affection, but shows no tenderness. Yes, it's a love scene, but love itself feels weirdly absent. Instead passion hardens into icy spite and mocking desire – a desire that manifests itself in anger or in humour. What looks at first extravagantly ordinary becomes on inspection intriguingly strange. What kind of film is this?

These scenes appear in Robert Hamer's *Kind Hearts and Coronets* (1949), Ealing's classic comedy of serial killing and class envy. Most famous for Alec Guinness's *tour de force* of playing eight roles in the same film, *Kind Hearts* is also one of the most sophisticated and sexy British films ever made. In it, Louis Mazzini (played by Dennis Price) murders, one by one, the members of his aristocratic family. In terms of style, it is unique.

The possibilities of living being limited, and life itself sadly brief, our first question must be why should anyone spend time watching *Kind Hearts and Coronets*, a black-and-white British comedy of the late 1940s? I hope that this book will answer that question, but before I begin, I'd like to give some provisional answers. *Kind Hearts* is a great work of art, and if art matters then it matters. It is very funny and, in a demonically subtle way, very wise. And for the bitter, the easy self-deprecators, the procrastinators, the snobs, the junkies of possibility, the flirts, the wits, the wastrels, the overly wordy, for all those it is perhaps the perfect movie. It is not a film for the humble or the dull. They are too good to need it. For the rest of us, it is both the disease and the cure.

. . . .

Before anything, *Kind Hearts and Coronets* is an 'Ealing film', and there would be no Ealing without Sir Michael Balcon. As producer at Ealing Studios, his vision gave a series of disparate movies the inimitable stamp of a house style. Though he certainly ended by thinking it the best of Ealing films, by some accounts Balcon began by hating *Kind Hearts*.[3] Why?

The answer lies in Balcon's personality, his beliefs and way of working. Born in Birmingham in 1896, he became one of the most successful British producers of the 1930s and 1940s. Balcon was a contradiction: an urbanite who played the country squire; an industrialist of cinema who preferred the cottage industry of Ealing to the lucre of Hollywood; a financial genius (he came up through the sales department) who was also essentially a creative producer.

Above all, Balcon was disillusioned with the USA. After a period working at Gainsborough, he had briefly made films for an offshoot of

Louis B. Mayer's MGM in London, among them *Goodbye, Mr Chips* (1939). Balcon hated the experience and soon left, moving to the newly vacated studios at Ealing. He had endured enough of the Hollywood version of Britain; now he would make British films for British audiences – instinctively knowing that this was anyway the best way to win over America: the more local the art, the more international its appeal.

Basil Dean's Associate Talking Pictures had opened studios at Ealing Green in 1931. In 1938, Dean returned to his old work in the theatre, and Balcon came to Ealing. ATP was soon forgotten as the company began to be known as Ealing Studios. They were outside the whirl of London, distant from competing studios in dowdy Shepherd's Bush or the slums of Islington. The atmosphere was village-like, countrified. Ealing was nominally independent, yet tied financially to J. Arthur Rank, the Methodist film mogul, and his British production company and cinema chain.

Unusually, almost uniquely, the films that were made at Ealing seem to belong to the studio or to Balcon, rather than to their directors. Any film buff knows that *Passport to Pimlico* (1949) is an Ealing film, but I would guess that only diehards could name its director. Sometimes, as in the case of *The Captive Heart* (May 1946), the publicity poster advertising the film gave Balcon prominent billing, while not even carrying the director's name (it was Basil Dearden).

Balcon guided film production at every stage: sometimes initiating projects; approving or vetoing scripts; actively involving himself in

creative decisions at production meetings; turning up daily to look over the shooting of the films. The studio believed in team spirit. Sometimes, it looked as though what that actually meant was Balcon as the paternalistic headmaster at a public school sternly overlooking the work of his errant boys. Genuine team-players could flourish in this set-up; others, among them Robert Hamer, the director of *Kind Hearts*, could lose out.

Nonetheless Balcon attempted something akin to democracy at Ealing, even if it were a democracy with hierarchical lunches, from the workers' canteen up to the executive dining-room for Balcon and his VIP guests. Yet to him the directors really were a team. Eyewitnesses talk of the directors' conferences, where they would all sit at a round table, drinking tea and thrashing out stories. The atmosphere was earnestly workmanlike: 'There were no big cigars and no self-important speeches, no condescension on the part of the big boss and no hypocritical lip-service from the men employed by him.'[4] At lunch times, the directors, writers and associate producers would meet and sometimes play complicated word-games, like some Senior Common Room that never actually existed: Angus Macphail, the screenwriter, could pass for a don, and Hamer might, had he not moved quickly enough, have become one.

Not all meetings meant drinking tea; the crew would head over nightly to The Red Lion pub opposite the studio gates. In such a set-up secrecy about a film in production was impossible; advice was freely given and received. The studio was run by committee; it was a 'family concern', and Balcon was undoubtedly the father.

Ealing wasn't just 'the studio with the team spirit', it was the studio with the team ethos. This was largely Balcon's creation, but does seem to

An Ealing film in production: on set for *It Always Rains on Sunday*

have been shared by the people who worked with him. The studio found directors within its own ranks – from the cutting rooms, or among the screenwriters. These men had grown up with Ealing and inevitably its spirit imbued them.

Moral rectitude was the first constituent of Ealing's ethos: Balcon specifically refused to make films that were 'socially objectionable or doubtful'.[5] Judging from Lindsay Anderson's book on the making of Thorold Dickinson's *Secret People* (1951) at Ealing, it's clear that Balcon's objections in script conferences are sometimes aesthetic (for instance, the worry that characters will seem 'planted'), but are chiefly moral. He expresses anxiety that the film will leave a sense of futility with the audience, and that 'the defeat of evil should be more externalized, made concrete'.[6] Balcon's taste was for 'the healthy type of story based upon actuality, for the non-erotic and unsensational'.[7] Immediately, we can see how the unhealthy, distinctly erotic and sensational *Kind Hearts* might run into trouble.

Second, the typical Ealing film carries a subtle political agenda, an unemphatic socialism. G. K. Chesterton once wrote of two kinds of democracy: the democracy of dignity, which touches on the common destiny and value of each human being; and the democracy of difference, expressing the ineradicable uniqueness of each individual, exemplified in the startling grotesques of Charles Dickens. Ealing films celebrate democracy of the Dickensian type. They breathe with the Little Englander's refusal to be homogenised, while nonetheless desiring to be part of the happy crowd. Difference, not dignity, motivates them; their forte is comedy, rarely tragedy. Ealing's were 'the films that beg to differ'.

Moreover, the team were middle-class Labour voters, quiet radicals, critical of institutions, yet affectionate about them too. Here Balcon describes their politics:

> We were middle-class people brought up with middle-class backgrounds and rather conventional educations. Though we were radical in our points of view, we did not want to tear down institutions. … We were people of the immediate post-war generation and we voted Labour for the first time after the war; this was our mild revolution. We had a great affection for British institutions: the comedies were done with affection. … Of course, we wanted to improve them, or, to use the cliché of today, to look for a more just society in the terms that we knew. The comedies were a mild protest, but not protests at anything more sinister than the regimentation of

the time. I think we were going through a mildly euphoric period then: believing in ourselves as having some sense of, it sounds awful, national pride.[8]

Balcon intended the films as safety-valves for antisocial impulses, limited rebellions against a status quo no one there really wanted to give up.

Third, the studio's ethos meant realistic portrayals of British life. This was one way in which Ealing asserted its independence, its difference, from Hollywood. Writing in 1946, Balcon was clear: the British documentary movement had enabled the British feature film to find its strength.[9] Ealing films would marry the sober traditions of documentary with the excitement of the narrative fiction film. In this way, Ealing could create a national cinema, projecting British values to a home audience and to the world.

At first, Robert Hamer seemed to Balcon an exemplary member of the Ealing team, enacting the studio's finest characteristics. And then, quite suddenly, *Kind Hearts and Coronets* changed all that.

. . . .

Evelyn Waugh declared that, 'We are all American at puberty; we die French.'[10] Robert Hamer was French at puberty; he died like an American.

There is an unfortunate myth that hangs around Hamer like the scent of stale whisky. The story goes that he's a one-hit director, hampered by a system that he was unconsciously trying to subvert, driven to alcoholism and an early death by the pressures of a career that never rose beyond its early peak. I would love to refute that myth. But I can't, for there is something true in it. But it is not the whole truth. It falls down in suggesting Hamer was a director with only one film in him. *Kind Hearts* really is a unique masterpiece, but the films that led up to it are fascinating, and some of what followed, for all its flaws, rewards close scrutiny.

How did Hamer fit into the cosy team at Ealing? The answer is complicated. In 1951, when a journalist from *Sight and Sound* sat in on one of the famed Ealing script conferences, he asked the assembled throng: what gives Ealing films their unity? Somehow this entirely expected enquiry stumped them. In the silence Hamer spoke, 'trying to formulate his thoughts while he has not yet finished thinking them':

> We are given complete liberty to follow our personal inclinations in choosing and elaborating our subjects. This seems to me a very

important point. Apart from this the explanation may lie in the fact that we all – as it were – belong to the same film generation and consequently have the same general approach. We have all started in Ealing and have shared the same experiences for at least 5 or 10 years.[11]

Hamer's response is interestingly contradictory. He stresses the worth of independence, not consensus; then puts the Ealing unity down to the fact of their common age and working history. In other words, Ealing's directors are free to follow their own path, but only because their environment means they all want to go the same way anyhow.

The moment implies a niggling tension in Hamer's position at Ealing, one borne out by the facts. Early on he was one of the studio's golden boys. Balcon particularly admired the fusion of narrative and documentary in Hamer's *It Always Rains on Sunday* (1947). After all, this was precisely the aesthetic he believed Ealing should pursue. In an essay called 'Realism and Tinsel' (1947), Balcon asserts his desire that Ealing forge a link between narrative film and realism. He wants the studio to make films that use realism to reconcile people to living in the everyday world, drawing them closer to a sense of its excitement and happiness.

A round-table conference at Ealing, with Hamer and Balcon

But two years later, it was not obvious that *Kind Hearts* was doing any of this. Perhaps this accounts for Balcon's anxieties over a film which is pure 'tinsel' – indeed celebrates theatricality, artifice and unreality – and which rejects the ordinary world as a very drab and dreary place indeed.

If Balcon acted the paternalistic headmaster, then he found in Hamer the classic example of a boy who breaks the rules to gain attention, even love, but only succeeds in alienating that love. It is an alcoholic's gambit: will you love me, even after *this*? In remarks made in an interview, Googie Withers appears to be speaking generally of Ealing's atmosphere, but I would guess that she's thinking especially of Hamer (the man who, after all, directed her in three of her five films for the studio):

> Mind you, there was something of the head-master in Michael Balcon; we almost leapt to attention when he came in. He was a funny fellow, very sweet with us, but he was also a moralist – didn't like any hanky-panky, yet he had all these men around him getting terribly tight all over the place! I think he knew how brilliant they were so he let them have their fun. Every single morning at 10.30 a.m. sharp he walked on to the

Balcon (seated on left) on the set of *It Always Rains on Sunday* with Hamer (in the scarf)   15

set as the producer. Filming stopped, and we stood there while he watched a scene or two; we would all say, 'Good morning, Michael', then he would go off again with a retinue of men behind him.[12]

Hamer's drinking took place in a situation where his work on set, and his drunkenness there, would be closely monitored. In a way, it was ideal; in these circumstances the apparently straightforwardly self-destructive act of drinking could find its external target: someone who would care, be hurt, reject him. Poor Hamer!

The institutional set-up at Ealing would have aided this infantile identification with Balcon as the unpleasable father. Hamer could play, to his heart's discontent, the serious artist, policed by the benign dictatorship of Balcon at the top. This isn't meant to suggest a facile contrast between Balcon the po-faced money man, and Hamer the incorrigible artist. Balcon brought an insightful and creative mind to the projects he produced, and Hamer, who had studied economics at Oxford, knew all too well the material basis of cinematic success: 'he has an unusual and valuable grasp of trade problems. He is therefore willing himself to accept concessions to popular taste if they will ensure the box office success of nine pictures in order to take a risk on the tenth.'[13]

So Hamer was that sad anomaly: the man who longed to be a team-player but who could not help being an outsider. He stayed with Balcon. And yes, Balcon admired him, although seeing him as 'probably at his best with the English indoors'.[14] Yet rumours persist that Hamer's life at Ealing was tougher than most. He reportedly couldn't make the follow-up to *Kind Hearts* that he wanted ('a story with strong sexual content set in the West Indies'[15]), so he temporarily left the studio to make the disappointing *The Spider and the Fly* (1949) for Rank. There's even a story, which I will describe later, that Hamer had a fierce dispute with Balcon over the editing of *Kind Hearts*.

Through his independence of mind and his drinking, Hamer became the seeming rebel who secretly loves to conform, which, of course, is exactly Louis's position in *Kind Hearts*. So it is that Hamer's life mixes establishment values and wilful choices. Born in Kidderminster on 31 March 1911, he was educated at Rossall (though he's sadly missing from the school's website list of 'famous old Rossallians'), and then on to Corpus Christi College, Cambridge, where he studied economics (and, by some accounts, mathematics as well) – with the intention of getting a job at the Treasury. So far, so predictable, but then that wilfulness kicked in and saw him, in 1934, begin work instead as a 'number-boy' at Gaumont–British. From here he progressed to odd-job man in the cutting room at London Films, then, to Ealing, working on many films, first as editor, then assistant director, then script collaborator, and finally associate producer on *San Demetrio London* (1943) and *Fiddlers Three* (1944). Hamer's break came on *San Demetrio London*, when Charles Frend fell ill with appendicitis, allowing him to step in temporarily as director. He followed this by directing brilliantly the mirror sequence in Ealing's classic portmanteau film of the macabre, *Dead of Night* (1945).

Pink String and Sealing Wax (1945) came next, a tale of adultery and murder in suitably sleazy Brighton, followed by his other lesser masterpiece, *It Always Rains on Sunday*. *Kind Hearts and Coronets* sealed Hamer's reputation as one of the leading Ealing directors. And then: almost nothing. Hamer's life thereafter becomes a story of mostly weak films and the ludicrously badly kept secret of his drinking. It's hard to say when the decline began. In 1943, Gordon Jackson knew of his problem while filming *San Demetrio London*, but at this point he was never noticeably drunk on set.[16] George Cole recalls that alcohol was already undermining Hamer's ability to direct by the time he was making *The Spider and the Fly*, the film that followed *Kind Hearts* in 1949.[17] When he directed his last film, the rather wonderful *School for Scoundrels* (1960), he was almost incapable of working. As Ian Carmichael recalls:

He was very, very unhappy because he had just been taken off the bottle. One was aware all the way through the film that he was being nursed along by the producer, an American called Hal Chester, who

The mirror story from
Dead of Night

used to pick him up every morning, bring him to the studio, and take him home every night to make sure he *went* straight home. He managed to last for about eight weeks. Then, when I came down for a night shoot in London, he was absolutely sloshed. The producer sent him home and directed that night's work himself. He then brought in a new director to finish the film, a man called Cyril Frankel, who never actually got a credit. In the weeks I did with Hamer, I felt that the *effect* of his alcoholism was on him – he was beyond his best powers.[18]

Hamer died, too young, in 1963.

Alcohol made Hamer 'a burden to himself and his devoted friends'.[19] Yet he was never short of friends to burden. The 1890s ambience of *Kind Hearts* and pictures of Hamer in dapper suits, colourful scarfs, holding a cigarette, may suggest a pallid aesthete in the director's chair. Actually he was a 'square, fair, [nearly] forty-year-old realist with his head screwed on'.[20] According to Alec Guinness, he looked and sounded like a scornful frog. He was modest, confident, witty. Another eyewitness describes him as unpretentious, certainly not precious or self-consciously arty.[21] This down-to-earth quality was essential to his technique as a director. By all reports, actors loved to work with him; he knew their frailties and understood their intentions. He was meticulous (he spent five weeks shooting the railway junction sequence of *It Always Rains on Sunday*), and in his best films often wrote the script and edited the film too. Descriptions of him directing *It Always Rains on Sunday* show a man attending chiefly to small technical problems and to the performances of his actors. Here is a slightly later description of Hamer's technique:

> Of the editor, Hamer has no fears, thanks not only to his own experience in the cutting-room, but also to his 'reactionary' refusal to go on the floor with a shooting script. His scripts contain neither cutting nor camera instructions. He goes on the floor and begins by rehearsing a scene in full. In the course of rehearsal, as the players 'walk through' their parts, he believes the cuts and camera angles proper to the scene become clear; while at the same time the method has the huge advantage of familiarity with the action when it comes to shooting out of continuity.[22]

Such a practical approach is unlikely to turn Hamer into the auteur once so beloved of film critics. Yet there are underlying auteurist patterns in his work: a powerful eroticism; a witty literariness; realism; guilt; doubleness; playfulness; and above all, the fate of a trapped protagonist hemmed in by the tiny possibilities that life offers. Hence *Pink String and Sealing Wax* ends with a suicide, and the more muted *It Always Rains on Sunday* closes with two characters who attempt to kill themselves, but aren't even allowed that small freedom. It's no accident that *Kind Hearts* should have rather a different relationship to the ability to forge possibilities in life. In every way, *Kind Hearts* responds to the realism and sense of entrapment peculiar to *It Always Rains on Sunday*. (Curious how that title should possess such seedy glamour, while being a near-comic quintessence of the dreary and downbeat in English life.)

The chief criticism of Hamer as a director, and of his work on *Kind Hearts* in particular, is that he's too wordy and lacks a visual sense. Lindsay Anderson said so in 1949, and critics have been saying the same thing ever since. It's as though Hamer were closer to Wilde than to Wilder. Actually this response to the film devalues its inspired cinematographer Douglas Slocombe, Hamer's cinematographer on his first four films as director. Slocombe was an educated and thoughtful craftsman, well aware of the theoretical implications of his work (as an article he wrote on Gregg Toland in 1949 exemplifies). Moreover, he photographed some visually stunning films: *Dead of Night*, *The Man in the White Suit* (1951), *The Servant* (1963), *The Great Gatsby* (1974) and Spielberg's Indiana Jones trilogy.

Yet perhaps even great cinematographers may lose out under a weak director. However, Anderson is wrong. He misses the essential secrets of Hamer's and Slocombe's visual style in *Kind Hearts*: its conscious theatricality, and its complex relationship to the film's reliance on the power of words.

Kind Hearts is Hamer's greatest film, and his chief claim on posterity. I have little sympathy with the auteur idea: films are collaborations first and foremost. Many others made invaluable contributions to *Kind Hearts*: Balcon; Michael Relph, the associate producer; Slocombe; the actors (Dennis Price, Alec Guinness, Joan Greenwood, Valerie Hobson); and above all John Dighton, the brilliant co-screenwriter for the film, Ealing stalwart and writer of *Went the Day Well?* (1942), among others. Without these people, the film would be utterly different, and probably much worse. Nonetheless it really is Hamer's film. For only Hamer could have directed it. Of all the Ealing directors, only Hamer experienced the allure of doubleness, the conforming rebellion of the outcast son.

But Robert Hamer was not the only one to hit heights in *Kind Hearts* they would never reach again. Dennis Price's career slumped from Hamer to Hammer. It was a decline accelerated, like Hamer's own, by contradictions between the public persona and the private man. As Price's life fractured, he went from leading British matinée idol to someone the *Sunday Mirror* termed, in its 1973 obituary, 'a knocked-about piece of cinema history'. Like Hamer, like Louis Mazzini, Price lived a double life, his 'true' self – heavy-drinking, gambling, gay – concealed behind the suave performance. He lived his life playing Dennis Price.

At times, the contradictions were unsustainable. Married to fellow actor, Joan Schofield (they met doing rep in Croydon), the marriage dissolved, after the birth of two daughters, in 1950. Then in 1954, he tried to gas himself in his Kensington flat. He was luckily saved by his landlady, Mrs Edna Lamb. A journalist for the *Daily Mirror*, with Hamerian innuendo, reported the background to the attempt. 'After a trip to his local, "The Hour Glass", Mr Cecil Charrington, the landlord, told me: "He came in gaily, cracking jokes. He had a few bitters with his friend, a chap

called Bobby, and they had a serious conversation. I didn't hear what Dennis said – I was too busy at the bar."' Wonderfully, Price supposedly said to the doctor on coming round from this suicide attempt: 'What glory, Price?' Wit in extremis is typical of his courage: in court for bankruptcy in the 1960s, when asked the cause of his failure, Price replied in true Louisesque fashion: 'I am afraid, extravagance.'

In 1961, when planning an autobiography, Price was characteristically downbeat about his own talents: 'I have no illusions about myself. I am a second-rate feature actor. I am not a star and never was – even in the old Rank days. I lack the essential spark, you see.' We may put this down to middle-aged disillusion. Yet in a publicity interview for *The Bad Lord Byron* in 1948, Price had already adopted this tone of world-weary self-deprecation: 'My dear, I'm just a cog in the machine. I do as my elders and betters tell me.'

The chief elder and better, the original from whom Price derived his true counterfeit, was Noel Coward. Price found himself as an understudy, a double almost, for Coward; his big break coming when jaundice (not a cold) allowed the understudy to take the centre stage, as he told a journalist in 1948:

> But I'm not only grateful to Noel for his cold. Not by any means. I learned more from that tour with him than I can ever hope to learn from anyone. How to deliver dialogue, how to concentrate on saying your lines. Coward taught me everything.

Price discovered his identity as an actor in the looking-glass of Coward.

At the time of his suicide attempt, the newspapers declared that Price, with 'his Regency personality', epitomised and burlesqued the role of the elegantly cynical villain. He only came alive on screen in the dandy's studied pose. From the beginning, critics were aware of Price's artificiality, his 'dry whimsy', that found its best expression in the character of Louis Mazzini.

Dennis Price being Byronic in Rome

The elegant young star during filming of *The Bad Lord Byron*

Price in drag in the terrible
Charley Moon

And there were other reasons why Price was the best, the only,
actor to play Louis.

Like Hamer, Price had followed and then deviated from the true
establishment career. Denniston Franklyn John Rose-Price, the son of
Brigadier-General T. Rose-Price, was born in Twyford, Berkshire, on
23 June 1915. He went to Radley and then on to Worcester College,
Oxford. Would the army follow, or even perhaps the church? But then
came the deviation: leading light in OUDS; drama school; rep; the West
End. In 1940, he joined the Royal Artillery, but was invalided out of the
army in 1942. From there, he went to work with Noel Coward, and then
broke into films in Powell and Pressburger's religious fable, *A Canterbury
Tale* (1944). Success had come to him; he signed to Rank, and appeared,
in 1947 alone, in eight films.

Success of one kind. In another sense, he was always failing, always
the son who had refused to follow the military career of his father and
grandfather. And he was queer. It is said that Price discovered his own
homosexuality while acting the bisexual Byron in the dreadful *The Bad
Lord Byron* in 1948. It is fitting, but unlikely, I think. Later in life he would
flirt with the possibility of coming out by playing 'gay roles': an actor in
drag in *Charley Moon* (1956); Robbie Ross to Robert Morley's Oscar
Wilde in *Oscar Wilde* (1960); and Calloway, a closet gay actor, in the 1961
thriller, *Victim*. And yet he never did come out. Like Hamer's drinking,
his homosexuality remained a partial secret, the twist that would keep
him living the double life.

. . . .

For most people, 'Ealing' now means 'Ealing Comedies', that run of eight or so movies, beginning with their precursor, Charles Crichton's *Hue and Cry* (1947), and ending with Alexander Mackendrick's *The Ladykillers* (1955). Only in June 1949, when *Kind Hearts* opened at cinemas in the West End, things didn't quite seem like that.

Ealing had always made funny films – vehicles for George Formby and Will Hay – and there had been the brilliant precedent of *Hue and Cry*. But before the summer when *Kind Hearts* was released, the studio wasn't at all known for comedy. It was the studio of sober realism. Michael Balcon's essay, 'Film Comedy' (written in 1948), alerted the public to a forthcoming change in direction at Ealing. He understood that filmgoers would be surprised to see Ealing making comedies, but reassured them that the studio would retain its realistic approach and the desire to give its films a 'social content'.[23]

In April 1949, Henry Cornelius's *Passport to Pimlico* came out; that June, Alexander Mackendrick's debut, *Whisky Galore!*, and then *Kind Hearts* appeared. Ealing Comedy was born.

Researching this book has meant immersing myself in the late 1940s, reading the long-forgotten writing of critics and film-makers.

A hilarious study in the gentle art of MURDER

The poster shows the women, but not Guinness

What one finds there is a peculiar earnestness – about film, about the working classes, about art. Even the fun exhibited by these men was that of schoolmasters letting their hair down at the end-of-term revue. They were industrious, liberal, tolerant, anti-dandyish, intelligent and often a little uninspired; roundheads not cavaliers; serious, all too serious. *Kind Hearts* is their antithesis.

For once the film historians agree. The third film released in that spring and summer of 1949, *Kind Hearts and Coronets* is the best of the Ealing comedies and therefore, by extension, the best of the films produced by Ealing Studios. On the film's re-release in 1964, the *New Statesman* critic declared it to be 'the most confident comedy ever to come out of a British studio'; in 1997, in the same magazine, Simon Heffer called it 'perhaps the best British film ever made'. The notable *Guardian* film critic, Derek Malcolm, put it on his list of the hundred greatest movies, seeing in it a rebellious combination of 'Wildean wit and the pessimism of … Marcel Carné'. In NFT programme notes in the early 1990s, it was 'the best of all Ealing films'; in *Forever Ealing* (1981), George Perry called the film Ealing's 'most perfect achievement'; and, most intriguingly of all, as already mentioned, after initial disapproval Balcon himself considered it to be his personal favourite. When compiling the list of 360 great movies that make up the BFI Film Classics series, David Meeker followed the general critical consensus in making this the only Ealing comedy. (And, apart from *Went the Day Well?*, the only Ealing film of any kind.)

Yet the critics agree about one other thing too. Raymond Durgnat declares that *Kind Hearts* 'in its suave, sharp insolence, is the most brilliant, and the least typical, of Ealing comedies'.[24] The German critic, Andreas Missler, concurs:

> *Kind Hearts and Coronets* is different from the usual Ealing Comedies: the film treats of the values of English culture in an angrier, more elegant, more cynical and less cautious way; it mercilessly exposes forms of behaviour, rituals and class differences without, however, reconstituting them in the end, as other Ealing films do.[25]

Early on, people sensed that the film was different. In 1951, Freda Bruce Lockhart writes: 'Most Ealing successes depend on story-idea rather than on treatment, on a fortunate blend of spontaneity, social conscience and cheerful vitality, rather than on style. Robert Hamer's approach to film-making, however, departs from the general pattern.'[26] This leads us to a nice contradiction: *Kind Hearts* is both the best and the least typical of the Ealing films.

Yet for the reviewers watching the film at its premiere on the very hot night of 13 June 1949, the film really did seem just another Ealing comedy – the third goal in a hat-trick of great films. They were generally agreed on its great merits, though some believed the joke wore thin, making the film drag at the end. Sometimes they pointed out the film's resemblance to Charlie Chaplin's *Monsieur Verdoux* (1947), another comedy of serial killing. More often reviewers compared the film to literary works – Oscar Wilde and Evelyn Waugh especially.

Yet there's some essential kink in Hamer's approach, some brilliance that confirms the sense of the film's difference. Some see this as a consequence of filming at Pinewood rather than Ealing, thus freeing a truant Hamer from the perpetually monitoring eye of Sir Michael Balcon. (Years later Balcon, probably wrongly, insisted that the film had been shot at Ealing.) The only danger in considering this atypicality is to imagine that because *Kind Hearts* (like Mackendrick's films) seems particularly undated, its date, its position in history, is of no interest in describing its power. As we shall see, *Kind Hearts* is a film embedded in a

26   Joan Greenwood (second from left) and Hamer (second from right) on set

specific moment of British history, as well as a work that explores perennial problems of living. But now perhaps the time has come to tell you the story that *Kind Hearts and Coronets* enacts.

. . . .

The film begins with a hangman arriving at the gates of a grim London prison. He is there to execute Louis D'Ascoyne Mazzini, tenth Duke of Chalfont. We first see Louis, in his prison cell, elegantly dressed, and engaged in writing his autobiography. Louis narrates nearly all of the film from now on as he reads from these condemned-cell memoirs. He relates the story of his birth, and the subsequent death by shock of his father (an Italian opera singer) on first seeing Louis as a newborn babe,

The memoirs begin ...

Louis's mother with the heart-shaped portrait

before moving back in time to tell how the D'Ascoyne family cruelly ostracised Louis's mother, a D'Ascoyne by birth, the daughter of the seventh Duke of Chalfont, for marrying beneath her.

In a series of brief scenes and images, we follow Louis's childhood in the suburbs of Clapham, the son of an adoring but snobbish mother, who only allows him to play with Sibella Hallward, the daughter of the local doctor. When he reaches the age of seventeen, Louis's mother applies to Lord Ascoyne D'Ascoyne, her uncle and a prestigious city financier, for Louis to be granted a job in his bank; but Lord D'Ascoyne refuses to acknowledge young Louis's existence, and the young man starts work instead as a draper's assistant. Unexpectedly a tram knocks down and fatally injures Louis's mother; as a final indignity the family refuse to allow her to be buried in the family vault. Louis decides to take revenge on the family by killing them, one by one, and so become himself Duke of Chalfont.

Made homeless by his mother's death Louis becomes a lodger at the Hallwards' house, where he is intimate with young Sibella, who, however, shows more interest in the very dull, but satisfyingly rich Lionel Holland. Nonetheless, Sibella clearly feels a strong interest in Louis. But desire for money wins out; she rejects Louis's proposal of marriage, having just become engaged to Lionel. This rejection hardens Louis in his resolve to murder all the D'Ascoynes. As a penny-tourist, he visits Chalfont Castle, the home of the eighth Duke, whom he briefly glimpses making a hasty exit from the hall.

Louis is working in a department store, when fate sends him his first victim. While buying clothes for his mistress, the supercilious son of

D'Ascoyne, the aristocrat, insults Louis, the draper's assistant

Lord Ascoyne D'Ascoyne, the banker, insults Louis, who is serving them. Louis stands his ground, is reprimanded for his insolence and consequently dismissed from his job. Deciding to take revenge, Louis pursues the illicit couple down to Maidenhead, where he contrives to kill both young D'Ascoyne and his amour by loosening their punt, as they make love on the river, and watching the two of them drift over the edge of a precipitous weir.

As subtle vengeance for the slight once offered by the old banker, Louis sends him a letter of condolence on the death of his son. The letter provokes Lord D'Ascoyne to extend an invitation to meet, which in turn leads to Louis after all securing a job at his relative's bank. On hearing the good news, Sibella experiences regretful desire for Louis, though the date of her wedding to Lionel is now fixed.

Emboldened by the success of the first murder, Louis decides to continue his plan, with the murder of Henry D'Ascoyne, a harmlessly pleasant chap and a keen amateur photographer. Under the guise of being another practitioner of this faddish art, Louis befriends Henry and is invited back to his house. There he meets Henry's wife, the beautiful but puritanically stern Edith. Asked to return for the weekend, Louis can commit his second murder, as he pours explosive in the drink that Henry is obliged to conceal from his teetotal wife.

Meanwhile, between his two visits to Henry and Edith, Louis surprises Sibella alone in the nursery at the Hallwards', weeping on the night before her wedding. Louis consoles her in the best way he can. Nonetheless, Sibella marries Lionel the next day, and Louis is on hand to congratulate the happy couple.

An invitation to escort the bereaved Edith to Henry D'Ascoyne's funeral enables Louis to see the entire remaining D'Ascoyne family together for the first time. After the service, the present Duke manages to upset Edith by his insensitivity, as he boorishly discusses the virtues of the family vault, and remarks on how he had to turn down the request of some man 'from Tooting or somewhere' to bury his mother there; Louis chivalrously steps in and ushers the tearful Edith away. In the carriage afterwards, Louis comforts Edith, and resolves inwardly that he will make her his wife.

Promoted at work, Louis moves out of the Hallwards' house and takes lodgings in St James's, then the traditional home of London's upper-class dandies. Despite his attachment to Edith, he encourages Sibella to visit him here, to distract her from her regrets and from the upsetting tedium of life with her husband.

Louis bides his time

Louis now embarks upon a series of murders, killing first, with a glass of poisoned port, the Reverend Lord Henry D'Ascoyne, whom he approaches while disguised as a colonial bishop visiting from Matabeleland. He then, with a bow and arrow, murders Lady Agatha D'Ascoyne, the notable suffragette, as she sails by in a hot-air balloon, dropping suffrage leaflets over London. The drowning at sea of Admiral Lord Horatio D'Ascoyne saves Louis the effort of this killing. He goes on to blow up General Lord Rufus D'Ascoyne with an explosive jar of caviare.

Saddened by this series of losses, Lord Ascoyne D'Ascoyne makes Louis a partner in the banking firm, for the young man is now heir presumptive to the dukedom. Emboldened, Louis proposes marriage to Edith. She gently refuses. The affair with Sibella continues. On one occasion Edith visits Louis at his rooms in St James's, just as he is expecting Sibella. She tells him that she has decided to accept his proposal. By appealing to the social proprieties, Louis persuades Edith to leave only moments before Sibella arrives.

Louis receives a message from Lionel, asking him to visit him at his house in Bayswater. There Lionel, drunkenly appealing to their childhood friendship when they were 'old pals', begs Louis for financial help as he is bankrupt and ruined. Louis refuses. Lionel threatens suicide, and then insults Louis as a counter-jumper, taunting him with the fact that his mother married an Italian 'organ-grinder'. Enraged, Louis slaps Lionel, and the two men fight, with Lionel even attempting to stab his 'old pal'. Victorious, Louis leaves Lionel lying abjectly on his sitting-room floor. Louis returns to his rooms, where Sibella calls on him unexpectedly. She pretends that Lionel has discovered their affair and declares that she wants a divorce so she can marry Louis, and become Duchess of Chalfont. Louis tells her that he knows she is lying, and that in any case he intends to marry Edith.

Edith and Louis visit Chalfont again. This time Louis goes as an invited guest. There he learns that the Duke plans to marry the dull but child-bearing Maud Redpole. If all his work is not to be lost, Louis must act quickly. Louis and the Duke go out hunting together, and Louis learns, after a disagreeable episode in which the Duke has a poacher beaten, that there are mantraps illegally set in the grounds. He carefully positions one such trap and on a second walk out hunting, leads the Duke into the trap and shoots him. On hearing the news of this last death, Lord Ascoyne D'Ascoyne, the banker, dies of shock.

We see Louis now as the gracious Duke of Chalfont, greeting his staff and tenants, but just at the moment of his apotheosis, the police arrest Louis for the one crime he didn't commit: the murder of Lionel Holland. At a trial in the House of Lords, Louis pleads his innocence, declaring that Lionel must have killed himself. But his story cannot match the widowed grief of Sibella, or the fact that no suicide note has been found. Louis's only consolation is that Edith, in an act of faith in his innocence, has married him in jail. His peers find Louis guilty, and sentence him to death.

On the eve of his execution, Sibella visits Louis, and suggests that his life might still be saved if a suicide note were to be found. Louis agrees, but points out that there is no such note. Sibella wonders if one might not, at the very last moment, by some miracle, be found; and also speculates on the possibility of Edith without warning, even miraculously, dying, leaving Louis, of course, free to marry again. Louis catches the hint. 'I'm afraid all this is going to take years off her life', he murmurs.

The memoir ends, with Louis still waiting for the note to arrive. The hangman comes to carry out the execution, when suddenly the prison governor indeed brings news of the suicide note's discovery. They release Louis, who leaves the prison gates to find cheering crowds, and Sibella and Edith, both waiting for him. Which one should he join? As he hesitates, a journalist from *Tit-Bits* steps up to ask him for publication rights to his memoirs. The very word is like a bell that recalls him to the realisation that he has indeed left his 'Life' in the prison, with all its incriminating words there. The film ends with a shot of the memoir's title page, left inside the condemned cell.

. . . .

The opening credits:
the family album

Not mentioning
Israel Rank

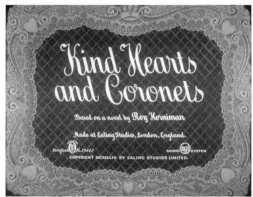

The wedding photo?

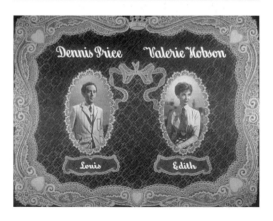

Suitably enough, as we shall see, *Kind Hearts and Coronets* begins twice, if not three times. The film first opens with the credits: they are tastefully stylised, beginning with a portrait gallery of the actors in the film, the photographs sentimentally framed in the Edwardian manner. Is this to be a film of quiet nostalgia? The music too is yearningly old-fashioned, an aria from *Don Giovanni*. Of that there'll be more to say later.

The film proper commences with the arrival by night at a grim London prison of the lugubrious Mr Elliott (Miles Malleson), the public executioner. Clearly, though this is the start of the film, we are close to somebody's end. Elliott's mournful enthusiasm for the approaching hanging establishes the film's black humour. This is to be his last job (another ending), the execution of a duke the 'finale to a lifetime in the public service', for 'after using the silken rope, never again will I be content with hemp'. However, Elliott feels some social anxiety: how does one address a duke? Could it be, 'Your Lordship?' 'Your Grace,' the Governor corrects him. 'Your Grace?' murmurs Elliott appreciatively.

And then we have our first glimpse of Louis. We see him from behind, the camera lingering on his neck. He rises; is courteous and reserved. His graciousness truly seems ducal. The Governor leaves, and Louis sits at his desk and opens his memoir, starting to read. And here the film begins again – indeed many critics ignore the little frame to Louis's memoir and mis-remember the entire film as told through the medium of his voiceover. In fact the memoir self-consciously marks a new start. Even within his memoir, Louis is uncertain about where he should start; time presses and there are so many possibilities: 'With so little time remaining to complete my story, it is difficult to choose where to begin. Perhaps I should begin at the beginning.' That beginning is Louis's birth, but it's also a kind of ending, for this birth causes his father's death, as papa succumbs to a fatal heart attack on first seeing the infant Louis. Yet even that won't quite do, for Louis's narrative now slips back before his birth and starts over again with his parents' first meeting, their falling in love, and the marriage that provoked his mother's exile from the aristocratic world of Chalfont Castle.

All this is very strange and very self-conscious. Why would Hamer and Dighton choose to open their film in this way, with these hesitancies and false starts? Two overriding sensations linger with the viewer. The first is that storytelling is a difficult and confusing art; there are just too many options! The second is that Louis isn't quite sure where he himself begins: is it the moment of his birth (also in some sense the moment of his

Louis ponders his memoirs

Louis's father expires

first murder), or back before his birth, with his parents' courtship and his mother's disgrace?

The film's origin is just as confused as Louis's own. In mentioning the opening titles, I omitted their only real oddity, namely that although the film originates from a novel, nowhere do they mention the title of that novel. *Kind Hearts* derives its story from *Israel Rank* (1907), written by the now almost completely forgotten Roy Horniman (1872–1930). For our purposes, the significant facts about Horniman are that he was almost certainly homosexual, and that socially he was a little adrift, lying somewhere between the respectable upper middle classes (his father was in the navy) and, on his mother's side, the Greek aristocracy. He was a productive, one-trick novelist, and one of the very few Edwardian inheritors of Oscar Wilde.

Horniman obviously intended the surname 'Rank' as a double pun, none too gently suggesting that his murderous hero is both a stinker and a social climber. The provenance of his first name is even more obvious. The hero's taint is Jewishness, which only social triumph will cleanse. The book is anti-Semitic in a meanly snobbish way, though undoubtedly also informed by the evolutionary racial theories so popular at the turn of the century. The only thing that would clear the book of accusations of anti-Semitism is to consider if Horniman was somehow on the side of his serial-killing hero. And strangely, it appears that he was. This is despite the novel being far crueller (and more angsty) than Hamer's film. Rank actually kills a child (something Louis by implication cannot do) by placing in his night clothes an infected handkerchief gleaned from another boy dying of scarlet fever.

Post-war sensitivity about anti-Semitism and their own moral sense meant that Hamer and Ealing avoid any mention of the film's source in Horniman's novel. (This sets aside the added complication that the film's ultimate financier shared the surname 'Rank'.) There had only too recently been a public relations disaster regarding anti-Semitism in British film. Alec Guinness's previous role as the caricature Jew, Fagin, in David Lean's *Oliver Twist* (1948) provoked riots on that film's release in Germany. The same movie was banned in Quebec, and only released in the USA in 1951 after twelve minutes were cut, in response to criticism brought by the Jewish Anti-Defamation League.

So why did Hamer opt for Louis Mazzini as the new name of his hero, and what was behind the choice of the film's ultimate title? To British ears, both Louis and Mazzini suggest the foreign, invoking the

The Nietzschean villain

myth that Italians are both more foppishly stylish and more vengefully murderous than the average Englishman. Notably, Edith and the D'Ascoynes own good old English names (the Duke is called Ethelred), while both Louis and Sibella sport suspiciously un-British names. Mazzini, of course, alludes to the famous Italian revolutionary and exotic foreigner on the London Victorian social scene. Maybe Louis's surname is Hamer's joke about Louis's own little revolution, as well as suggesting that upsetting the social order doesn't quite stop him enjoying its finer fruits.

The film's title might have been suggested by a memory of E. F. Watling's recent play of the same name (1937), a work derived from George Colman's *The Heir at Law*, the subject of which is the rise of 'simple, "middle-class" folk … into the unfamiliar altitudes of rank and fashion'.[27] More directly, the title comes from the Tennyson poem, 'Lady Clara Vere De Vere', itself quoted by Edith in the course of the film:

Trust me, Clara Vere de Vere,
From yon blue heavens above us bent
The gardener Adam and his wife
Smile at the claims of long descent.
Howe'er it be, it seems to me,
'Tis only noble to be good.
Kind hearts are more than coronets,
And simple faith than Norman blood.

The poem describes a commoner's refusal to fall in love with an aristocratic woman, after she has prompted another young suitor to kill himself for unrequited love. The poem's subject alludes to class tensions in the film, while the sentiments about true nobility lying in goodness, and the virtues of simple faith, are clearly apt. Moreover, one suspects that both Israel Rank and Louis Mazzini would have found Tennyson pompous, official and therefore intrinsically funny.

What drew Hamer to Horniman's novel? T. E. B. Clarke, Ealing screenwriter, remarks that Hamer was already thinking of a comedy of murder in the immediate post-war period, intending to make a film on Landru, the French serial killer.[28] Chaplin's *Monsieur Verdoux*, based on the same case, put an end to that. A reissue of Horniman's novel published in 1948 came to Hamer's attention, and he saw that it contained 'the germ of a film'. That germ may have been pointed out to him in Hugh Kingsmill's fascinating introduction to that new 1948 edition of

Charlie Chaplin in
Monsieur Verdoux

Israel Rank. Most likely Hamer's film offers a critique of Horniman's novel seen through Kingsmill's eyes.

Kingsmill describes his adolescent passion for Horniman's book on reading it shortly after its first publication. After World War II, he found the book again and re-read it with curious feelings:

> The book was even more brilliant than I had remembered and, considered solely as a thriller, seemed to me a flawless masterpiece, its variety of incidents being strictly subordinated to the grand simplicity of its central theme, the murder of the six persons who stand between Israel Rank and an earldom. The many and the one, and the one slowly and surely absorbing the many – it was as though one were watching the working out of a mystical experiment.
>
> Since *Israel Rank* appeared in 1907 a similar experiment has been attempted by the person whom our press during the Munich period used to refer to as 'the mystic of Berchtesgaden'. Hitler, unlike Israel Rank, did not succeed with his experiment, for it is not in the nature of things that the mysticism of evil should triumph in the end. *Israel Rank* is therefore essentially untrue; it is a daydream in which reality is shaped to the heart's desire, a vision of the kind of world a good many people were trying to believe in during the last years of the nineteenth century and the first decade of the twentieth.[29]

The implication of Louis's Nietzscheanism and even incipient Nazism may seem far-fetched to some. I'm not so sure. Think of how Louis callously breathes a sigh of relief as the Duke of Chalfont's twin sons die

37

of diphtheria. The indifference to the sufferings of others is, in a small way, Hitlerian. Think of those very funny gags delivered, James Bond-like, over the deaths, and the exclusion of real pity that they wittily represent. The hero is in Kingsmill's words, the 'apotheosis of the complete egotist':

> It was, however, neither Horniman's wish nor within his power to give a true picture of the course taken by untrammelled egotism. On his own level he was an exponent of the will-worship which on a much higher level ruined Wilde and on a higher level yet drove Nietzsche mad; and having a very considerable talent he converted his dream into a brilliant entertainment.[30]

First-person narration perfectly displays such a character's incuriously cruel egotism, as Nabokov was soon to demonstrate in *Lolita* (1955). (Had he seen *Kind Hearts* before he wrote that troubling, wonderful book?) Kingsmill bequeathed Hamer a striking view of his hero, and in the process suggested a possibility for his own film.

. . . .

Already fatherless, Louis soon loses his mother in the tragic tram accident near Clapham Junction. We see Louis kneeling at her bedside, his mother played with dignified sorrow by Audrey Fildes. Fading, she requests burial at Chalfont's family vault. She dies, dropping in that instant from her frail hands the heart-shaped photograph of her dead husband. Louis weeps uncontrollably.

The sentimental death-bed vigil

Put like that, it sounds like a death-bed scene from a drearily sentimental Victorian novel. After all, what could be more heartfelt than a mother's death? Yet the moment is not like that at all. Louis's posture appears faintly ridiculous; the pair seem arranged in a tableau. The photograph drops clunkingly, and there is an air of theatrical awkwardness. Most of the scenes of emotion in the film are like this, as though they were slightly out-of-place quotations. There is nothing particularly funny about any of it, and yet the off-key effect is undoubtedly comic. You want to laugh but you're not sure why. Maybe there's nothing intrinsically funny about Clapham Junction, or trams, or mothers, or death. The humour comes from the feeling that we are not seeing life, or even the representation of life, but rather the parody of that representation. The film knows your objections to such scenes, in art, as well as in life. Yet such scenes do happen, and isn't it just like living in its most self-conscious mode to pause and catch behind each event the shadow of how it would look as art? The film appears to concern snobbery in class terms; it is just as much about snobbery in art. It looks down upon the entire world of 'second-rate' artistic taste.

Balcon apparently told Hamer: 'You are trying to sell that most unsaleable commodity to the British – irony. Good luck to you.' Irony pervades the film, and accounts for its unique flavour. Debates about the uncinematic literariness of *Kind Hearts* really come down to this. It is a film about words (Hamer declared that language was the key to the film), but here words become a uniquely cinematic device, married to an image and undermining both words and image. Both become mere surfaces. The meaning of that surface is style. And the meaning of that style is self-conscious disdain.

As I have already said, reviewers frequently sought literary antecedents for the film: Max Beerbohm's *Zuleika Dobson*, Jane Austen, Oscar Wilde, Lytton Strachey, Harry Graham's *Ruthless Rhymes for Heartless Homes*, even De Quincey's essay on 'Murder as One of the Fine Arts'. The reviewer for the *Sunday Dispatch* specifically compared the film to the 'sort of leg-pull Evelyn Waugh or Stella Gibbons might have devised'.[31]

The literariness is there in the little quotations and parodies that Louis scatters across the film. The famous lines about shooting an arrow in the air and Lady Agatha falling to earth in Berkeley Square mock Henry Wadsworth Longfellow's moving short poem, 'The Arrow and the Song'. That the original poem should be both genuinely affecting and therefore a slightly embarrassing piece of Victorianism is of course the point. The whole film is a straight-faced parody of Victorian art forms, emotions and proprieties. Valerie Hobson, undervalued for her part in the film (precisely because she was so good at what she set out to do), makes the point eloquently:

> I did two high comedies with Alec Guinness, *Kind Hearts and Coronets* and *The Card*, which were, I think, two of the most elegant British comedies made. I have always thought the main reason for the success of *Kind Hearts and Coronets* was that it played absolutely dead straight, very seriously. It's a matter of being aware that you are playing a funny situation, yet playing it so straight that even the tongue-in-cheek doesn't show. Robert Hamer, the director, a genius, who died sadly young, was a very sophisticated man. To play something that requires sophisticated handling, you cannot have a naive director.[32]

The humour is therefore consistently deadpan: think of the smoke rising behind Edith's shoulder unobtrusively signalling to Louis that Henry D'Ascoyne has met his explosive end. The film is not going to tell you that this is a joke; it requires your sophistication. Like Austen, Hamer does not make art for such dull elves that cannot work the meaning out for themselves.

The film's use of innuendo in this regard is crucial. Another meaning – be it sexual, murderous or snobbish (and the film collapses the differences between these three) – hides in the surface of language. Some innuendoes were edited out in England: in the uncut version, Louis gave Lionel a wedding present of antlers (the old cuckold joke). In America,

A killer emerging from under water

even more were cut, including the gag about the girl who dies with young Ascoyne ('I was sorry about the girl, but found some relief in the reflection that she had presumably, during the weekend, already undergone a fate worse than death'). Some were left in. There's Louis congratulating Lionel at his wedding to Sibella with the words, 'You're a lucky man, Lionel, take my word for it.'

In two ways then, the film plays with the surface of things, using both double entendre and a continuous subtle sense of the parodic to suggest that we should never take what we hear and see straight. The film expects you to be knowing. Yet it shows that knowingness is a misfortune, an illusion, a fault. When, early in his fortunes, Louis tries to 'make love' to Sibella, she rebukes him with the accusation that he's 'playing the stage lover'. That thought is intrinsic to the film. To the acutely self-conscious everything one says or does can feel like the playing of a part, the acting of a conventional role.

....

Shortly after his mother's death, Louis embarks upon his first murder. He follows the caddish young D'Ascoyne and his anonymous mistress (in the script, she's simply known as 'The Girl') down to a little hotel in Maidenhead. In the hotel gardens, Louis irritatingly introduces himself to the erring couple, but they brush him off, naturally preferring to be alone. Late on Friday afternoon, they discreetly slink off to their room. It is annoying, if understandable, as Louis reflects: 'I deprecated their retiring so early, but it was hard to blame them, for weekends, like life, are short.' Louis waits all evening for them to come down. And the next

Taking the air (and plotting murder) at Maidenhead

morning. And that afternoon. And the evening too. They finally re-emerge from their room late on Sunday afternoon, leaving only just enough time for Louis to kill them.

This is, in its understated way, one of the clearest references in British film up to that point to the fact that a sexual life exists. If in *Passport to Pimlico*, sex is out of the question because you can never be enough alone, here the bright surface of the film calmly alludes to a privacy elsewhere, a room that you can never enter (much as the couple rebuke Louis's intrusion).

Sex permeates *Kind Hearts* if you have an eye to see it. It is easy to miss much of it, not really taking in Sibella's frustrated wish to be having sex with an unspecified number of Italian men while away with Lionel on their disappointing honeymoon. Do the illicit couple that Louis kills actually die while having sex? Hamer had brought sexual themes into each of his three earlier films. Here Googie Withers, the leading actress in all three of them, reflects on Hamer:

> Robert Hamer used to try very hard to get around the rule that you had to have one foot on the floor in a scene with a couple on the bed. Although in *It Always Rains on Sunday*, I was in bed with Edward Chapman (my husband in the film) reading the Sunday papers, we were almost fully dressed, with the covers pulled up. Sex was very understated in films, then, and your imagination took over, whereas now ... I think it was *much* better when it was left to your imagination.[33]

In *Kind Hearts*, the proprieties of cinema insist that the sex takes place off screen, fixed only in our minds. Wonderfully, it's this that ensures the film's erotic power. Sex becomes a matter of speculation, the one thing not turned into the parodic second-hand of representation.

The sexual theme depends upon the Hardyesque contrast between two women, one apparently sexless, the other extremely sexual. The film presence of Joan Greenwood is crucial. Born in 1922, Greenwood was one of the sexiest of all British actresses. Her eroticism lived in her voice: husky, breathy, purring, insinuating, engrossing, flirting, always promising. Audiences had recently enjoyed her as the love interest in *Whisky Galore!*, as Lady Caroline Lamb erring with Dennis Price as Byron in *The Bad Lord Byron*, and in *Saraband for Dead Lovers* (Basil Dearden, 1948), scripted by Dighton and Mackendrick, another film about illicit love. She was marking out her territory as the bewitching other

Hamer filming the passion of Googie Withers in *It Always Rains on Sunday*

Joan Greenwood, sexily vivacious in *Whisky Galore!*

woman. Louis admires Sibella for her imperfections, for the fact that she is vain, selfish and adorable. Like Louis, she lives in an emotional chill. As in the film itself, sex and deception are the only things that warm her.

. . . .

After murdering Ascoyne, Louis sends, as a polite relative should, a letter of condolence to his victim's father. It is an impeccably courteous gesture. And it is Louis's subtle act of revenge against Lord D'Ascoyne for 'his cruelty to Mama'. The dish best served cold also turns out to be remarkably nutritious, since, young D'Ascoyne being dead, and a vacancy therefore having arisen, the letter leads to a meeting with Lord D'Ascoyne and Louis's consequent employment in the bank. An act of pure spite, enacted as an exemplary show of decent feeling, works just as though the courtesy were genuine. Sometimes we have to be kind to be cruel.

Manners exist so we may clothe our selfishness and hostility in the garb of good actions. When we are conventionally polite, we nearly always act better than we are, using social constraints to raise us above ourselves. However, the conventions mean that an act performed in a spirit of genuine goodness may seem identical to one that hypocritically cloaks the vilest enmity. If the mannerly man is a good actor – and Louis is a very good actor indeed – then the potential to deceive becomes endless.

On returning from his propitious meeting with Lord D'Ascoyne, Louis encounters Sibella waltzing alone around the nursery. They dance together to the mantelpiece, and pause. She has news: she has accepted Lionel's proposal of marriage. Louis congratulates her, and then, beautifully, corrects himself: 'No, I should congratulate him. I compliment you.' The film is a veritable etiquette guide: an aspiring socialite would do well to imitate Louis, who has the *noblesse oblige* that the nobility conspicuously lack. And now it is his turn to tell Sibella something: he informs her of his new job. Sibella softens and pouts, inviting Louis to show with a kiss that he has forgiven her for ever doubting his link to the D'Ascoynes. He bends over her to kiss her, flinches, and stops himself. Alas, it would, he tells her, be wrong for them to kiss after her pledge to Lionel. It is another act of sweet revenge as Louis masks with moral rectitude his intention to wound her for the rejection he has suffered. These are the points around which the film revolves: a blow to one's *amour-propre*, a show of manners, and revenge.

The engagement with being seen to do the correct thing (as Louis remarks to Sibella, during their clandestine affair, 'these things only become wrong if people know about them') is more than just another instance of the film's essential coldness. Reviewing the nearly contemporary Ealing drama *Scott of the Antarctic* (December 1948), and feeling little patience with its stiff-upper-lip heroes, Lindsay Anderson wrote of how that film avoids all passionate feeling: 'When emotion threatens, make your characters talk about something else in a little, uncertain, high-pitched voice.'[34] Anderson likewise imagined *Kind Hearts* as 'emotionally quite frozen', confusing one kind of Antarctica for another. The coldness in Hamer's film is not stoical, but cynical; it is the coldness of desire and hate.

Partly that coldness was a consequence of Hamer's directorial preferences. As Alec Guinness points out: 'He disliked close-ups, he liked distancing things. ...'[35] Yet the apparent remoteness, the distance put on people, enables the dissection of their natures. In a *Sight and Sound* article, to the puzzlement of his interviewer, Hamer affirmed his fascination with character:

> The impact of one character on another, the strange human patterns made up of often irrelevant characters; these, he declares, are the things he tries to put on the screen. Evidence of this preoccupation is not easy to find in the films so far.[36]

Really? Actually, Hamer drops a large clue here to the true subject of *Kind Hearts and Coronets*. In the same interview, Hamer quotes Zola's defence of *Thérèse Raquin* ('J'ai simplement essayé ce que fait un chirurgien sur deux cadavres') as a credo for what he longs to achieve on the screen.

In the brilliant and chilly atmosphere of *Kind Hearts*, character reveals itself within the proper conventions of social life. Louis, in particular, insists upon the proprieties, using them, for instance, as a way of distancing himself from Edith, even as he pursues her. (The whole courtship, in which a killer seduces the widow of the man he has killed, replays Richard III's wooing of Lady Anne in Shakespeare's play.) Edith cares less than Louis himself for the restrictions that manners dictate. She declares: 'There are some conventions which must be governed by individual circumstances.'

Louis's endorsement of social conventions forms part of his engagement with the appearance of things, with the style in which they are done. *Kind Hearts* will never go out of style. For, fittingly, style is its essence, the mode by which it engages with the world. In this film Hamer hit a note that continues to resonate through contemporary British culture. The detachment and distance that once made the film an oddity now seem central to what post-war art involves. Its scepticism and parody of innocence continue to resonate. We cannot talk about this film without talking about ourselves.

The film appears to endorse an aesthetic, and not a moral, sense of people. In *Kind Hearts*, it is not goodness or badness which determine our sense of someone's worth, but their dullness or their interest. Lionel's greatest sin is being boring. Somehow it strikes us as aesthetically right that he should erase himself in suicide. No viewer of the film ever worried over Lionel's death. Even his decision to live in Bayswater, dire evidence of bad form, seems sufficient reason for his hastily self-inflicted demise. When Louis begins his memoirs, the film flirts with the anxiety that they might prove tedious. From then on, avoidance of boredom provokes all its energy, its irony, its perfect instinct for malice.

Lionel is far from being a symbol of goodness. Edith might be, and she's both a prig and a source of refined fascination for Louis. We might profess to despise this amoral preference for excitement over the supposedly dull weight of goodness. And yet, doesn't modern culture depend upon the allure of the wicked, of the exciting even if it is wicked?

For Hamer, the choice of the aesthetic over the ethical carries one further resonance, intrinsic to *Kind Hearts*, but easier to spot in his last film, *School for Scoundrels*, based on Stephen Potter's *Oneupmanship* books. Here Raymond Durgnat describes the *modus vivendi* of that film:

> Professor Alistair Sim (long-time headmistress of St Trinian's) presides over an academy which teaches its adult pupils how to upstage, over-awe, bruise, crush, obliterate and expunge, with apparently impeccable politeness, the egos of all rivals in the universal rat race.[37]

As far as it goes, this is accurate enough. But it misses one crucial thing. The real inner sense of that film, and of *Kind Hearts* too, is that life is a game. And a game for winners. Louis embarks upon social life as someone who knows the rules, but feels fully prepared to cheat at them. He has lost the sense of what the rules are for. But what does it matter anyway? And, as for the audience, we all prefer a cheat to a spoilsport; for at least they still play the game.

. . . .

It is one of the foremost ironies of a film where style rules that the class to which the eminently stylish Louis aspires should be so drab. The film depicts the D'Ascoynes as cads, boors or buffoons. They bore others and they bore themselves. Their anecdotes are boring, their tales interminable. The endless free time they have bores them and so they take up pointless, boring hobbies (photography, shooting etc.); and the Duke of Chalfont is so bored by his prospective wife, Maud, that he decides to take her abroad until she is confined to the castle by pregnancy: 'No sense inflicting her on one's friends.' On the other hand, Louis is that thrilling thing, 'an aristocrat who fulfils the aristocratic ideal'; only he's no aristocrat.

Louis pursues a double desire, both embracing and despising the aristocracy. Concentrating on only one side of the contradiction, critics have argued for simple class readings of the film. Ealing comedies, they affirm, are fantasies celebrating the middle-class hero. Even those readings which stress Louis's unlikeness to the typical Ealing protagonist go on to flatten out the film by suggesting that Louis is the champion of a broadly socialist attack on an outmoded feudal order, even if that attack is itself evidence of a murderous attraction. Others simply describe the film as though it were *Passport to Pimlico*, similarly revealing Ealing's endorsement of community solidarity against bureaucracy. In this analysis, both films – all Ealing comedies – become expressions of lower-middle-class Utopian desires.

Kind Hearts' class allegiances are far more subtle than this. In fact, the whole point of the film, in these terms, is the ambiguity about the class to which Louis belongs. Does his upbringing define him, or his parentage? Should he be placed by where he begins (a draper's assistant) or where he ends up (a duke)? Simplifying things distorts them. It would be ludicrous to argue that because Louis works in a shop he is therefore working class; or that the audience are meant to endorse his attack on the aristocracy (an institution which his murders will help him join). Louis's placelessness, his moving between classes, forms the source of his interest.

To understand *Kind Hearts*, we need to keep the political context in mind. A Labour government was in power, elected in a landslide victory in 1945, inspired by egalitarian impulses provoked by the war. After this Labour triumph disillusion set in, much of it created by the period of austerity enforced by the expense of the war; above all, rationing was still in force four years after the war itself had ended.

Hamer's politics were broadly left wing. *It Always Rains on Sunday*, the film he made before *Kind Hearts*, has been seen as both a bowdlerised version of Arthur La Bern's novel, and 'a last, brave attempt by Ealing to grant the working-classes the recognition they were felt to have earned during the war'. After that,

> the feeling seemed to be that only little stories were needed to illustrate the simple sentiments, the a-to-b emotional gamut, the narrow little lives, of 'ordinary people' (a phrase which all but enabled the shabby genteel and the 'respectable' working-class style to edge the ordinary working-classes out of the picture altogether).[38]

In *It Always Rains on Sunday*, Hamer undoubtedly sought to portray 'real' working-class life, thereby defending British culture against American influences. The Ealing directors fetishised Britishness; here was something Hamer certainly shared with Balcon.[39] John Collier's book on the making of *It Always Rains on Sunday* shows an embarrassing and patronising concern on the part of the film-makers not to embarrass or patronise working-class audiences. The desire to make things (such as 'working-class speech' or 'working-class interiors' with their 'atrocious designs') real and 'essentially typical' painfully reveals the pious awkwardness these Oxbridge graduates and middle-class Labour voters actually felt around working-class people.

From all this, Hamer comes across at this time as left-thinking and earnest, and not at all someone who would next go on to make *Kind Hearts*. Unless, that is, *Kind Hearts* is more political than I appear to think, or less political than Hamer himself hoped? But I do think the film political. It certainly engages with class, but does so in unexpected ways.

There's the complexity of Louis's class position. There's the fact that, despite great wealth and prestige, by 1949 the upper classes were really finished as a political force (the end of a process that had started even before Horniman began his sinister little novel). There's the contemptuous affection shown to the aristocracy in other films made at the same time as *Kind Hearts*, like the good-natured *The Chiltern Hundreds* (1949), in which the aristocrats have become what they are to us now – bumbling eccentrics who are overly dependent on their servants.

There's the interesting question of casting. Valerie Hobson as Edith was an inspired choice, playing off as it does on the relation to her previous role as Estella in David Lean's *Great Expectations* (1946), another 'posh' girl looked up to by an aspirant male. Even better (looking forward to a strikingly similar casting tension in Nic Roeg's *Performance* [1970]), lower-middle-class, illegitimate Alec Guinness plays the rich

Masters and servant in
The Chiltern Hundreds

Valerie Hobson as Estella
with John Mills as Pip in
Great Expectations

D'Ascoynes, while the genuinely upper-middle-class Dennis Price, son of a brigadier-general, plays the impoverished social climber.

In this film aristocracy is merely a performance, and Louis is simply the best performer. Aesthetically speaking, he deserves the role. That aristocracy should in truth be no more than a surface, a style, leads us to the point where the film's deepest relationship to class appears: that is, in the matter of clothes.

Living in Britain after the war, Evelyn Waugh would refer to England under the Labour Government as 'the occupation'. Would the socialists obliterate the hallowed class system, with its carefully stratified layers of money, manners and prestige, with gradations based on endlessly complex and often mysterious distinctions? Actually, no, they wouldn't. At the time, no one knew that; old certainties appeared on the point of vanishing. Some, like Waugh, expressed their hostility in print. But there were other ways of responding.

Kind Hearts appeared just as Edwardiana was defiantly, nostalgically fashionable among the newly irrelevant aristocrats and upper middle classes of the post-war period: Old Etonians, Guards officers and adolescent ex-public schoolboys about town. The key figures were men like Bill Coats, Bill Akroyd, Mark Gilbey. In 1948, dispossessed by the triumph of the Labour government, they began to dress in the styles of 1907, the year of Israel Rank.

The New Edwardians were a Savile Row phenomenon (Hardy Amies was a key figure), young Guards officers returning to civilian life and exchanging:

> their military uniform for another kind of uniform. They all still looked exactly alike, wearing clothes which were a direct echo of the masculine modes of the early years of the century. In this there was an undoubted element of nostalgia. Since all clothes mean something, these meant: 'I wish I could go back to an epoch when men of my class had all the advantages – chambers in Jermyn Street, a man-servant like Jeeves and an income from investments, which, if small, was assured.[40]

They dressed as though it were still the golden age of the aristocracy, and as if the lost Edwardian years really were that golden age (which they were not). There was a wider passion for the Edwardian period at the time – you can see it in the novels of Ivy Compton-Burnett or L. P. Hartley – and this fashion was just a part of it. The New Edwardians (as they were called) were Keith Douglas's unicorns, living in a mythic dream of history. They were startlingly absurd. The look was extravagant, dandyish, as:

> from about 1948, guardsmen and bloods began to appear in long and narrow, single-breasted jackets and narrow trousers; turned-back velvet cuffs and velvet collars on overcoats; carnations, patterned waistcoats and silver-topped canes ... By 1950, the Edwardian Look had become the dominant London fashion.[41]

For the first audiences watching Louis, he would have seemed not just an exotic hothouse dandy, an outlandish Oscar Wilde; Louis was in the height of fashion. In terms of the way class works in *Kind Hearts*, the meanings of his clothes had been carried over from the New Edwardians on the streets of St James's and Mayfair into the process of the film. Anthony Mendleson, Fulham-based costume designer for the film, must have known all about the latest fashions and their desirability for London audiences still constricted by the clothes ration. Most people were still wearing utility clothes, and this after the long war years, when there had even been a government ban on trouser turn-ups.

The film defines Louis's ascent through his clothes: as he rises up the social scale, his clothes similarly gain in extravagance, beauty and elegance. How drab they are in Clapham! And how very elegant, once he has moved to the West End. Louis's dandyism is an energy, a mark of the

Lionel the drab ...

... and Louis the elegant

vitality that distinguishes him from the dowdier bodies of the D'Ascoynes. Having been sacked as a draper's assistant (a significant occupation in this context) he spends the last of his wages on suitable apparel for Maidenhead, acquiring stylishness just as he commits his first murder. His battle with Lionel over the exotically attired Sibella manifests itself just as much in the wildly disparate dress sense of the two men as it is in their brief fall into physical violence.

However, the progress of the New Edwardian look after the film's release reflects the larger meanings of Louis's sartorial presence. The social tensions embodied in these clothes uncannily parallel the film's own involvement with class and style.

These class concerns are more than neutral engagements with the dandy, with Oscar Wilde and Max Beerbohm, with Dorian Gray and Vivian Gray, with Byron and Beau Brummell – as if such slanted images of Englishness as queerly 'cutting a figure' were ever neutral. In fact, the film expresses something central to London life in 1949. The ways in which New Edwardian styles merged with the dress codes of notable gay upper-class men imbue the film, focusing as it does on the Byronic style and reserve of gay man, Dennis Price.

As implied, the first transformation of the New Edwardian look– and this probably predates the release of *Kind Hearts* – occurred when it was flamboyantly taken up by visibly gay Londoners, particularly Neil 'Bunny' Roger. Roger brought colour and tightness to the look – in particular wearing astoundingly tight trousers. He made an upper-class fashion into a queer fashion; leading it to be discarded, even at the height of its dominance, by the straighter Old Etonians. The next move in the history of this fashion is even more unlikely.

In its engagement with street fashion, *Kind Hearts* is inescapably a London film. Living in London, perhaps any major city, it is hard to escape the imprisoning feeling that the rich have privatised beauty; that they have appropriated the means to graciousness. In London (in the drab suburbs where Louis grows up), you soon grasp that ease and elegance exist in streets you can merely walk through, in houses you'll never own or maybe even enter. Since World War II, beginning with the Teddy boys, clothes and street style have become a quixotic protest against the ugliness of your parts of the city. Clothes offer the possibility of living the life of the star or the aristocrat you dream yourself to be. Even for middle-class kids, living in sterile comfort, and lost in *nostalgie de la boue*, London still contains its areas of secret desire. The other worlds they aspire to are those dirty but 'real' working-class places their parents would have disapproved of: the clubs, the pubs, the racetracks, the football grounds. These too can be zones equally distant and equally open to the thefts of the imagination.

So the look moved from Savile Row to the East End, and up to Tottenham, Highbury, then on to Streatham, Battersea, Purley, Shepherd's

The dandy of St James's

The dandies of Ladbroke Grove (photo: Roger Mayne)

Bush, Fulham, and then everywhere. The New Edwardians became the 'Teds'. Caught in a dream of the self as immaculate, as living in the cushioned world of the metropolitan rich, working-class young men appropriated the look of upper-class nostalgic dandyism. They stole a beauty and a style that existed elsewhere; their clothes aspired to something. They would be someone. The working-class Teds donned the dandyism of the St James's aristocrats. This dandyism was narcissism, of course, taking the self for its own love object, adorning and celebrating its own body. And wasn't that Louis's ultimate end too? Didn't he too dream of himself as perfect, complete, always effortlessly elegant?

The New Edwardian/Ted moment most visibly manifests the post-World War II world of social mobility. Louis's ascent more than parallels theirs. It is the primary version, a prototype that thousands were to follow.

The last stage for the Edwardian look was being borrowed by middle-class, art-school kids longing to be working class, just as the first Teds had longed to look posh, and the Guards officers had longed to rewind the clock of history. Clothes and post-war style were not classless, but were rather a place where class longing and contempt and anxiety could be reinvented as resentful, tender fantasies of belonging. And always happiness exists in some tangible but ever-shifting elsewhere – in some other group, or some other time. For Louis, happiness means owning Chalfont Castle, so removing his mother's disgrace.

The film's approach to class moves far beyond the stereotypical and weary obsession displayed in so many other British films of the period. In *Kind Hearts*, class is wit, brio, a manner of dressing, a gesture, a way of living in the surfaces of things. The film is at its most outrageous and its deepest as it collapses this surface into a strangely inflected joke about the possibility of grace.

. . . .

The middle section of the film pursues two parallel courses: the wooing of Edith, the widow, and the affair with Sibella; and Louis's murder of each of the D'Ascoynes.

It's difficult to unpick whose decision it was that Alec Guinness should play the entire D'Ascoyne family, chiefly because almost everyone involved with the film claimed credit for it. Perhaps the ultimate source was Hugh Kingsmill's already quoted hint about *Israel Rank*: 'The many and the one, and the one slowly and surely absorbing the many – it was as though one were watching the working out of a mystical experiment.'

In the theatre, the doubling of minor roles by the same actor was commonplace; and even in cinematic terms, the idea was far from a unique one. Most significantly, two of the three Dighton-scripted Will Hay films (all made at Ealing) involved Hay playing more than one role, or at least disguising himself variously: in *The Black Sheep of Whitehall* (January 1942), Hay had adopted six different disguises, two of them female; while in *The Goose Steps Out* (August 1942), the comic had doubled up, playing both himself and an enemy spy. (By the way, as George Perry points out, the Dighton-scripted *My Learned Friend* [June 1943] anticipates *Kind Hearts and Coronets* in having an inept Hay battling against a serial killer working through a list of victims.)

In *Kind Hearts*, Guinness plays eight roles, as well as being the original for the portrait of the first Duke of Chalfont, and perhaps also for the first duke and his wife in effigy on the family vault. It's tempting to feel that the multiplication of Guinness's roles in *Kind Hearts* responds to this actor's chameleon nature. The advertising poster for *Kind Hearts* shows the other three stars of the film as they appear in the

The Guinness gallery

title sequence: glimpsed in an Edwardian photo book; the space for Guinness's photo remains empty. Kenneth Tynan's appreciation of Guinness in *Harper's Bazaar* (April 1952) cogently delineates the actor's unique qualities:

> Facially, he is akin to what John Locke imagined the mind of a newborn child to be – an unmarked blank, on which circumstances leave their casual trace. Guinness looks bland and unmemorable, and will never be the average man's idea of an actor.[42]

The impersonations in *Kind Hearts* are a *tour de force*, nearly a mode of self-transcendence for an actor renowned for his insecurities, his adolescent dislike of his own appearance, his desire to escape from himself.

Yet it is crucial to the film's meaning that Guinness's disguises are such that they fail to conceal the ever-recurring features of the actor's face. Guinness is not really lost in each part, but only found once again. And this gallery of quirkily different but fundamentally similar characters strikes to the very heart of the film's weird appeal.

The doubleness, as in the multiple casting of Guinness, finds many echoes in the texture and narrative of Hamer's films. Hamer had a fondness for such structures, the suitable aesthetic counterpart to his own

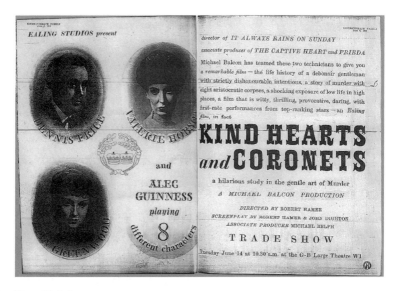

double life.[43] He returned to the double-casting ruse with the sombre *The Scapegoat* (1959), where Alec Guinness plays both an English university lecturer and his double, an impoverished French count. The doubles technique appears more subtly in *School for Scoundrels*. There doubleness is the basis of the plot. Terry-Thomas and Ian Carmichael play rival suitors for April (a happily symbolic name), in a story in which everything happens twice (two trips to the office; two visits to a car salesman; two tennis matches, and so on) and in which the end of the film similarly repeats its beginning: Terry-Thomas going, as Ian Carmichael had at the movie's start, from the railway station across the tracks to Lifemanship college.

In *Kind Hearts*, the idea of doubleness begins with the retrospective narrative, the story told through Louis's memoir. Events are both described and witnessed, and the sense persists that what we see on screen as the present is already the past, a completed action caught between the past tense of the memoir and the present moment of film.

There are so many other clues: the fact of serial killing, with its insistence on repetition; the two boxes of chocolate given to Sibella by her lovers; the two visits to Chalfont Castle; the repeated nursery love scenes; the sight of Chalfont in watercolour, the shot dissolving to an image of Chalfont in reality, doubled in its representation. Frequently the process of doubling works in terms of dialogue as well. Actors repeat lines; things are said twice or more. Let's take some instances, first a minor one. In his rooms, Louis asks Sibella how she has enjoyed her honeymoon: '"Not at all." "Not at all?" "Not at all."' The echoing is witty; each time the actors repeat the phrase it carries a differently charged meaning. Likewise there's the immediate recapitulation of Louis's little love speech listing Sibella's adorable imperfections. Or the reiteration of the words, 'Your Grace' at the beginning of the film, or the word 'memoirs' at its end. Or we could think of Lionel's repetition, picked up with distaste by Louis, of the unhappily sentimental phrase 'old pals'. Or the words 'a matter of some delicacy' which Lionel similarly fetishises, and the policeman who arrests Louis significantly repeats. All this might just be a verbal tic, or bad writing. I don't think so. Hamer makes the film do these things, subtly drawing us into a world of duplications, echoes and resemblances.

The whole process perhaps begins with *Israel Rank*'s own doubling of Wilde's far superior *The Picture of Dorian Gray* (1890) (itself a double of Huysmans's *A Rebours* [1884]), the model that Horniman adoringly copied. Israel/Louis glances back to the doubleness of Wilde himself, his addiction to social prestige and sexual slumming, as Kingsmill again implies:

> But a passion for social distinction and a taste for practices [gay sex? murder?] penalised by society are closely interrelated, for society has a peculiar fascination in the eyes of those who are violating its code, the appetite for its favour being intensified by the fact that it may at any moment be withdrawn.[44]

The question of Horniman's homosexuality, and Price's, returns to haunt us here.

The D'Ascoynes in image and in the flesh

The aristocratic D'Ascoynes only appear together once, at the funeral of Henry D'Ascoyne, in a 'trick shot' that attracted its share of admiration at the time. That the meeting should occur at a funeral is, I would guess, deliberate. As the Reverend D'Ascoyne remarks to Louis (disguised as the colonial bishop), here, at the family vault, the dead watch over the living.

The multiplying of Guinness into all the D'Ascoynes subtly diminishes the possibility of pity or outrage around the murders; Louis's enemy is not a person, but a family, and there are just so many of them. And yet behind that erosion of our sympathy lurks another more nightmarish sense that each murder is the same murder; that there is a series of the same person; that we are watching the mystical mathematics of murder, even of genetics.

The film bears witness to the biological principle that underlies the aristocratic system. It offers a bizarre tribute to heredity. Hence the same endlessly repeated features, the dead metaphorically (all but literally) watching over the living, not only from the stultifying locale of the vault, but in the mirror's revelation of the family face. The message is clear: belonging to the family means belonging to death. It is because Louis's dead mother cannot join them in the vault that the killing begins. One even feels that the family themselves are deathly, even cursed, as Lord D'Ascoyne speculates.

In this mirror of heredity, all the aristocrats really do seem one person. The family face (itself a kind of doubling) is the face which Louis does not possess. Instead he inherits the face of the father – the father who is the ultimate source of his, and his mother's, ostracism. Every son may feel that he is simply a second edition of his father, a belated double. All the major male characters (and also Lady Agatha, the childless, husbandless suffragette) are played by two people: Price or Guinness. Only wives (Louis's mother, Sibella, Edith, the King's courtesan, Maud Redpole) come from outside the confines of the two opposing male lines. And these women only exist as brought-in breeders. As the Duke of Chalfont remarks about Maud, his prospective wife: 'Good breeding stock, the Redpoles, and they litter a high proportion of boys.' The line snags on that bestial word, 'litter'.

The actor is always a double, being both himself and some imaginary other. And though *Kind Hearts* may be most famous for Guinness's many roles, we should remember that Price too plays two parts: Louis, the son, and the father (as well as appearing in disguise as the bishop of Matabeleland). Like the D'Ascoynes he is a chip off the old

Alec Guinness as Lady
Agatha …

… as Admiral Lord Horatio

… and as General Lord
Rufus

block, another instalment of the family face – as passed on by the male line. Although, and the film curiously insists on this, unusually the D'Ascoynes can inherit the title to the dukedom through the maternal line: 'Had she lived, your mother of course would have succeeded before you.' But she is dead, and Louis, already enjoying the mad omnipotence of the orphan son alone with his mother, can act out revenge for this abandonment by killing the members of her family, at once asserting and eliminating the D'Ascoyne element in himself.

But Louis can never erase who he is; nor can he find his identity ('the Duke of Chalfont') through the act of murder. Price is both father and son; so, sadly, is Louis, a young man who, having killed (as a baby) his own father, becomes 'a second son' (having killed the real son) to the bereaved father, Lord D'Ascoyne: criss-cross. Louis's belatedness, his resemblance to someone lost (a father, a son) is only another way in which the film asserts to us that a beginning is never really a beginning, your identity is never really your own, never originating with you, no matter how good an actor, how much of a self-inventor you are. Everything Louis does is just the shadow of his parents' loving transgression.

I have saved the clearest instance of doubling for last. For Louis desires two women, and his vacillations as he fails to choose between them counterpoint his multiple murders of the D'Ascoynes: 'Sibella was waiting for me when I got back. I was pleased to see her – for while I never admired Edith as much as when I was with Sibella, I never longed for Sibella as much as when I was with Edith.' The two women are physical opposites, embodying that Shakespearian comic split between a tall and a short woman, as well as representing the two class poles of Louis's life – Sibella's suburban chic versus the grand rectitude of Edith. Perhaps it's wrong to invoke Shakespeare; if anything the contrast is Hardyesque, even Lawrentian: two women, one cerebral and sexless, the other carnal and erotic.

With such a contrast, it's hard not to favour Sibella over Edith. Most people do. Recently, Gore Vidal has suggested that Hamer himself was in love with Joan Greenwood, but thought he couldn't have sex with her, as she'd teasingly told him that she was 'too small to be entered'.[45] The details feel unlikely, though the story might be true, making Greenwood even more convincingly the object of illicit desire in the film. Moreover, as Catherine de la Roche pointed out at the time: bad girls make good box office.[46] However, even good critics like Lindsay Anderson have missed the subtlety of Valerie Hobson's performance:

Kissing Sibella …

… and kissing Edith

Only Valerie Hobson, as the lovely widow of poor Henry D'Ascoyne, fails to make anything of her opportunities; hers is a part of outrageous arrogance and priggishness – with pride she quotes to Louis her late husband's testimonial to her: 'You have too much good in you for one man. I sometimes wish that others could have a share in it.' Miss Hobson plays without any apparent consciousness of the implications of her lines, and succeeds in making Mrs D'Ascoyne as boring on the screen as she would be in life.[47]

I don't think Anderson knew what a high compliment he was paying Valerie Hobson in that final sentence. Of course, to show her consciousness of the 'implications' would spoil the gag. Also he misses the dual meaning of Henry D'Ascoyne's line: both that she is too good for Henry (she's a prig), and also that she's a woman who ought to have other men. If that was an unconscious wish of Henry's, it's one fulfilled by the film. However, Louis and Edith's marriage presumably remains unconsummated as the film closes, due to its being solemnised in prison. It's right to bear in mind that at the end Louis hesitates between familiar Sibella and a first night of passion with Edith.

What's vital about all this is that it shows that sexual motives are as important to Louis as class ones. According to the critic John Ellis, this was the source of Hamer's strongest disagreement with Balcon when it came to the editing of the trial scene. Balcon considered it overlong. But Hamer fought hard to keep the film as he had written it, sending passionate letters to colleagues, canvassing support against Balcon in a way unprecedented at the studio:

> Eventually a compromise cut was agreed on. From the slender evidence provided by pre-production and release-print scripts in the BFI Library, the argument seems to have hinged around a very different interpretation of the entire film. In the trial, Hamer apparently wanted to emphasise the sexual nature of Louis's prevarication between the cold aristocratic woman and the smouldering doctor's daughter. Balcon wanted to emphasise the social nature of the conflict, with Louis's prevarication being between two classes ('the people' or 'the ruling class') with the women exemplifying this choice for him. The final cut keeps elements of both. This difference and Hamer's attempts to involve the whole senior staff show how his attitude differed from the studio's general approach. Usually sexual matters remained at the periphery of Ealing films; Hamer's battle was to make them more central to the film.[48]

I'd guess the sexual element was so vital to Hamer not just because he felt an emancipated desire to liberate stuffy Ealing. It's because we cannot understand Louis without it.

Louis is one of those men who only wants to be with someone else's wife. In the course of the film, Louis replaces three husbands. The first, his father, he accidentally kills by being born; the second, Henry D'Ascoyne, he actually murders; the third, Lionel, he is accused of murdering. It's easy to see this desire to be in another's place as Oedipal: the German critic, Missler, and Charles Barr do. Critical circumstances impelled Barr into arguing, against Lindsay Anderson's accusation of its coldness, that *Kind Hearts* is 'warm' exactly because it is Oedipal and erotic. Actually, Anderson seems closer to the truth: it is *cold*. But that's its virtue; it portrays a cold Oedipus complex, a cold eroticism.

The reader's heart perhaps sank at the mention of Oedipal complexes. Don't fret. The film clearly uses this theme, but does it in ways that are beautifully original and strange. This is not simply an Oedipal film, but a Darwinian one, a story for the post-DNA generations. Also the Oedipal here is, as in *Hamlet* (and Louis quotes Hamlet), a parable of the actor. And finally, the erotic manifests itself in an ironic addiction to artifice, a refusal to inherit straight the artistic conventions passed down to us. Doing so, it plays with the surface of things, content to divorce itself from the expression of actual passion.

To point us in the right direction for understanding Louis, Hamer uses Mozart's *Don Giovanni* as the music that Louis's father sings. The 1940s vogue for Søren Kierkegaard and the very recent first publication in English of *Either, Or*, with its brilliant analysis of *Don Giovanni*, could be behind this. For Louis is the Don Giovanni of murder and his own Leporello, keeping a list of his victims, addicted to the open aesthetic of possibility.

The aria that Louis's father sings, 'Il mio tesoro intanto', is Don Ottavio's vow of revenge against Don Giovanni, for his treatment of Donna Anna.[49] Its first verse, asking that Donna Anna should be looked after, is appropriate for Louis's father, bequeathing her as he unwittingly does to the care of his son. The second verse with its vow of revenge for the wrongs suffered by a woman is of course completely fitting for Louis's project of murder against the D'Ascoynes. Without even taking

Dennis Price as Louis's father

on the Don's 'Oedipal' killing of the ineradicable Commendatore, the song alludes to both roles that Dennis Price plays, uniting in an instant both son and father.

Louis may be a passionate revenger: certainly the only moments of spontaneous anger in the film occur in relation to his mother being slighted. And clearly his sexual fascination for both Edith and Sibella derives much of its energy from that revenge. Yet no one watching the film could fail to be struck by Louis's oddly disengaged love for both Sibella and Edith. Louis is Baudelaire's dandy in love. With Edith, he is cool, restrained, dignified and (in a un-Freudian sense) repressed; with Sibella, he is sarcastic, remarkably unpossessive, as much interested in the wound to his *amour -propre* as in the loss of her when she chooses Lionel. That's a quintessential male split between woman as moral instructress and woman as sexual obsession. We feel the pain of his failure to choose between them, without ever once taking it as the tragedy it undoubtedly is.

. . . .

The sequence of murders ends just as Louis seems temporarily to have decided between his two women. Engaged to Edith and estranged from Sibella, Louis takes a trip to stay at Chalfont Castle. There he discovers that the Duke plans to marry Maud Redpole, chiefly, as already described, for her capacity as a 'breeder'. On a hunting trip, Louis kills the Duke, having first trapped him in one of the estate's own illegal mantraps. While the Duke struggles, Louis tells him how he has killed six D'Ascoynes (actually he has only killed five) as revenge for the way the family treated his mother, and that he is now going to kill him. He

A tragic hunting accident

carefully positions himself with the shotgun and murders the Duke. Of course the camera does not show us the instant of the Duke's death. Yet for a moment we are brought face to face with Louis's brutality; he really is killing people.

It is a scene in which our residual connection to Louis might evaporate. So how does Hamer negotiate our sympathy for our hero?

Many things work together to lessen the heinousness of Louis's crimes. There's the grotesque nature of his victims, underlain by the fact that they are all being played by the same actor. There's their boorishness and boringness. There's Louis's attractive wit and style. Also there's the essential artifice of the film. We accept the murders because they are unreal, a mere 'graceful arabesque on murder', a 'grim subject for comedy, but one rather relished by the English sense of humour'.[50] When a film depicts violence so fancifully, as only a kind of art, then it is easy to ignore the fact that it is nonetheless violence.

Yet, close to the end of the film, Hamer gambles with losing our sympathy for Louis, by showing us his murderousness with unprecedented clarity. The sudden change in tone made the reviewer for *The Times* see the scene as a blundering lapse in taste, both 'brutal and shocking'.[51]

All the previous murders are more plainly comic – the poisoning of the vicar; the shooting down of the balloonist-suffragette; the on-screen exploding of the general and the off-screen exploding of the photographer; the drowning of the philanderer and his 'innocent' mistress. Louis occasions one more fatality after the shooting of his host, when the news of the Duke's death causes the heart attack of his banker employer and surrogate father. This is a death that Louis might feel morally responsible for, but in terms of the movie as a viewing experience, I would guess that few people in any given audience worry about his complicity. That the death of this pseudo-father should resemble the death of Louis's actual father – both men dying from shock – is undoubtedly no coincidence, as already suggested.

Hamer both risks and invites our shock at the death of the Duke. Yet the Duke of Chalfont is the most repellent of all the family that Louis murders. If the others are caddish, ineffectual or guilty of the sin of being boring, then the Duke is in addition outrageously rude. His insensitive comments to a grieving Edith at her husband's funeral reveal a positively aggressive lack of imagination. On the other hand, Louis always demonstrates perfect tact. On the first hunting excursion, we witness the Duke's cruelty to the poacher, whom he orders his servant to beat in the film's most disturbing act of violence. Louis responds to the thrashing ordered by this local tyrant with barely suppressed horror. (He's already declared himself to be too sensitive for blood sports.) In fact, in the brief instant that we get to see Louis in action as the aristocrat that he always wanted to be, it really does seem that, unlike the man he murders, he will make a magnanimous and caringly patriarchal Duke.

In her interview with the director, Freda Bruce Lockhart indicates that while Hamer intended the Duke to be hateful so as to garner sympathy for Louis, the plan backfired as 'audiences took the old buffer to their hearts'.[52] Personally, I find that incredible. Yet if it were the case, that itself would be interesting. The Duke's actions are ghastly, but they are hardly capital offences. Who can say who actually deserves death?

Well, Louis can. It is a deft touch that has Louis reciting to the Duke the real 'reason' for his death: not the Claphamite's social ambitions, but revenge for the unfeeling ostracism of his mother. That hardly excuses what Louis does, but it certainly provides a motive. We have only just now seen the Duke dispensing his own illegal justice by trapping and thrashing a poor working man; now Louis similarly dispenses his own brand of illegal justice. The two family members are playing by the same rules; it just so happens that Louis plays that little bit harder.

Hamer probably liked the idea of the kind-hearted killer. Compassion for the criminal, and a resentful contempt for the process of the law pervade both *Pink String and Sealing Wax* and *It Always Rains on Sunday*. In Louis's last murder, Hamer may really have been hoping that the audience gain a sense that for him killing is a kind of justice. He may have wanted us, as he wrote later in 1959, when we sit in judgment on our fellows, to: 'Fill the seats of justice with good men, but not so absolute in goodness as to forget what human frailty is.'[53] A contemporary critique of *It Always Rains on Sunday* had complained of its 'crook with a kind heart'[54]: did Hamer remember those words when he came to make his next film, responding to the lack of sympathy in the reviewer's complaint by making a film that would really explore and test the depth of the kindness in our hearts?

. . . .

Louis stands trial for the one crime he did not commit, the murder of Lionel. Contemporary reviewers tended to see the trial scene as the weakest episode in the entire film, an unaccountable lapse of form. And the scene is indeed odd; an anticlimax and not the great set piece we hoped for. Yet the apparent weakness of the trial scene clarifies Hamer's darker purposes still further.

As we've seen, Hamer was primarily a director who loved to work with actors. And in *Kind Hearts*, a film whose central conceit is that aristocracy is a mode of performance, he produced a film really made to exhibit the excellence of actors. In an otherwise unsympathetic review, *The Daily Herald* realised the film's great strength: 'I cannot imagine any actor or actress doing less than rave about it, and I cannot imagine any considerable mass of the paying population doing more than think: "Ah, well. They do like their bit of fun, don't they?"'

We should think of Louis primarily as an actor. Louis is always playing a part, whether it's that of the stage lover, the photography enthusiast, the colonial bishop, the perfect gentleman or the concerned friend. At the moment of Louis's arrest, this expression of his personality in the public role of actor becomes most clear. The discrepancy between screen image and voiceover is at its sharpest here. Fresh from making his speech to his servants and tenants, Louis is confronted by Inspector Burgoyne of Scotland Yard. Inside our hero is in turmoil; outwardly he looks self-possessed and wonderfully calm, still bowing and smiling to the enthusiastic crowd. Here as elsewhere, Louis's acting allies the courtesy of manners to the deceit of hypocrisy. The hiddenness of social life and the hiddenness of acting are really the same thing. Both suggest a process by which small gestures, telling words, positive actions, reveal character. Yet the character revealed is a fiction; in that very telling phrase, it's a game of make-believe.

This celebration of the actor's craft overlaps with, but is not quite the same as, the film's elegant and ironic wit, its exploration of the

Louis on trial

resources of English. And this is the key to the strangeness of that trial scene. Louis is a kind of Oscar Wilde, the actor of private life, and we fully expect a scene like Oscar's finest hour on the witness stand. We want Louis to give himself up to magnificent invective and witty rhetoric. Instead Louis appears robbed of words, decisive but inarticulate, his replies mostly confined to monosyllabic expressions of agreement or dissent. And as the prosecuting counsel runs rings around our perplexed hero, finally he traps Louis into stunned silence.

Counsel interrogates him about his relationships, accusing him of killing Lionel lest Sibella's divorce should wreck his chances with Edith. Louis vigorously disagrees:

> CROWN COUNSEL: Still you were proposing to discard Mrs Holland?
> LOUIS: No.
> CROWN COUNSEL: Even though you were about to be married to the other lady?

Louis hesitates, unable to find any reply, 'perceiving the trap into which he has been led'. But it was truly a trap that he set himself. Questioning drew him into the centre of the paradox in which he lives, unable to choose finally either Edith or Sibella; unable to choose.

There are other scenes where Louis's protective web of words breaks apart. In a film about serial killing, the fight between Louis and Lionel is the only scene in which anger becomes palpable. Here again language collapses. Although the inadequacy, the dullness, of Lionel's words are one point of the scene, he still has the power to sting Louis out of his verbal power by alluding to his mother's social position. Again, when confronted with something that genuinely disturbs and touches him, Louis loses his cool, and, more importantly, his eloquence. (Only minutes before, when Edith accepts his proposal, Louis tells her, 'You rob me of words.')

Unexpectedly inarticulate at his trial, Louis suddenly becomes that most pathetic of things: an actor who cannot remember his lines. And just as Louis's performance fails, Sibella's magnificently succeeds. She plays the grieving widow with effortless mastery, even allowing the careless wound of a little pause before finding her tears. She simply outclasses poor Louis.

Louis's only joke in the whole trial is his line about the alleged circumstances of Lionel's death, in which Louis as jealous lover supposedly killed the husband of the woman he loves. It is, he tells the crown counsel, 'one of the clichés of the cheaper kind of fiction'. The film itself could never endorse so cheap a fiction; yet the prosecutor dismisses the real story, as we have seen it from Louis's memoirs, as hilariously unlikely. The cheap fiction wins out. The author of that fiction is Sibella.

With regard to the position of women, *Kind Hearts* is the most egalitarian of all Ealing films. It's the only one to grant the role of villain to both the leading man and leading woman. Sibella is Louis's double – they deserve each other. Both of them are artists of real life, manipulators, storytellers, deceivers: actors. As Louis has killed so many, so Sibella will happily kill him – or Edith: whichever is more convenient. She plainly guesses the real reason for Louis's ascent to the dukedom, and says nothing of it to the police. Although only Louis faces execution, the two of them are in the same boat: 'Now if only you'd married me instead of Edith,' she says to him. 'Or if only you'd married me instead of Lionel,' he says to her.

Remember how Sibella tells Louis to stop 'playing the stage lover'; the line tells us as much about her as it does about him. Both of them are always acting; both make up a story for themselves. And that means they are making a story for the other. The relationship between them is a battle of storytellers. And at the trial, Sibella triumphs. Dependent on cheap fiction as it may be, her narrative defeats Louis's. You can be too ironic about second-hand literary conventions. Sometimes it's best to remember their power.

And her victory reveals the terrible fragility of Louis's performance. When the wit goes, only incoherence remains. The voiceover memoir is just a surface too; its words guarantee nothing but their own rhetoric. They don't reveal the truth; they reveal the constructed personality that is Louis: not a nature, but a performance.

In the preface to the edition of the film script, John Russell Taylor approvingly describes Louis as a dandy of words.[55] That's right, but what would it mean? Louis intends his words for narcissistic display. What matters to him most is the polished surface. Their depth might seem to come from the hiddenness of the murders. Only to us those aren't hidden. What we get is a beautifully crafted sophistry: 'you can always count on a murderer for a fancy prose style'.

Louis is a man without depths. His meaning exists on the surface: of clothes, of manners, of wit. When the mask slips, only anger and inner confusion appear. Behind the apparent politeness is the real confusion of evil: the evil that cannot distinguish one woman from another, or one victim from another. The film brings together a love of the surface (the well-litness of the film is its ironic undermining of film noir – evil is best understood in the light) and the use of the supposedly 'literary' device of the voiceover (actually a cinematic coup). Both are ideal expressions of Louis's shallow, empty evil. The film's love of style, the way in which everything shrinks to a style, is actually the moral meaning of the film. This is what happens, it tell us, when everything becomes just style: murder becomes a comedy; people become things. And in believing that, Louis is us all: the modern flirt; the addict of cool.

. . . .

Louis and Sibella have one more scene to play. When she visits him at the prison, they talk of the 'if onlys' of their life: if only she hadn't married

Louis behind bars

Sibella behind bars

Lionel; if only he hadn't married Edith; if only he were still free; if only a suicide note had been found. If only a miracle could happen. The miracle that Sibella arranges for Louis – the finding of Lionel's suicide note – strikes a bargain for the miracle that Louis implies he will arrange for her – the tragically early demise of Edith. In *Kind Hearts*, the 'if only' of art, of desire, can become theirs through the practice of the art of murder:

> LOUIS: So we now have two miracles in mind, do we?
> SIBELLA: Yes.
> LOUIS: I wonder if they are in any way dependent on each other?
> SIBELLA: I suppose perhaps they might be. What do you think?
> WARDER: Time's up.
> SIBELLA: What do you think?
> LOUIS: Poor Edith! I'm afraid all this is going to take years off her life.

That their bargain should merely be implied is the last and most perfect instance of the film's reliance on our – and Louis's – knowingness. When Sibella, testing her lover, asks him repeatedly 'What do you think?', she plays into the film's preoccupation with the hiddenness of thought, its revelation in polite social life only through the subtlest indications, the most indirect hints.

The joke about the 'miracle' and the curious insistence on Louis being addressed as 'Your Grace' mark a further level of irony in the film. Britain in the 1940s experienced, in terms of art and culture, something of a Christian revival. This was the era of C. S. Lewis's apologetics and Tolkien writing *The Lord of the Rings*; the novels of Graham Greene and Evelyn Waugh; the detective stories of Dorothy L. Sayers; the discovery of Kierkegaard and Simone Weil; the paintings of Cecil Collins and Stanley Spencer; the poetry of T. S. Eliot and W. H. Auden; the cult of personality around Charles Williams. In films, too, an undercurrent of Christian feeling is frequently discernible: Catholic Hitchcock; the anti-materialist fantasies of Powell and Pressburger, particularly in *A Canterbury Tale*, Dennis Price's first film; coming over from America, Frank Capra's fantasy of small-town miracles, *It's a Wonderful Life* (1946); and, above all, Carol Reed's *Odd Man Out* (1947), and his Graham Greene collaboration, *The Third Man* (1949). Add to this the fact that Dennis Price had briefly considered entering the church, that Alec Guinness was soon to convert to Roman Catholicism, the religious themes that Hamer would explore with Guinness in *Father Brown* (1954),

Dennis Price looks for a
blessing from Eric Portman
in *A Canterbury Tale*

Religious imagery in *Odd
Man Out*

and it's clear that the film's religious interests – so easily lost – are in fact
intrinsic to its context and its concerns.

Guinness tells us that T. S. Eliot disapproved of *Kind Hearts* on
moral grounds. It's likely that he scented the air of parody around the
idea of 'grace', the mockery of the miraculous. While Carol Reed's
Christ-like killers struggle for their little bit of grace, Sibella's plotting
hints that the miracles celebrated in the films of the time are just another
cinematic illusion, just another kind of fiction. Her made-up miracle
displaces the hangman's words of religious fear and indignation, and
that's just another story being silenced – like Louis's at the trial, like the
general's interrupted and too-often started tale of his adventures in the
Boer (bore) War. 'It is a miracle,' the governor cries. Louis murmurs

knowingly, 'Yes, it is like a miracle,' – much as he is like a duke, and his feelings for Edith and Sibella are like love, resemblance here being close enough to the real thing.

The miracle that Sibella makes is not God's, but her own. It is the improvised miracle of her art. She manifests hiddenly her prowess at drawing the story to her own ends.

And so, still awaiting his execution, Louis's memoirs likewise end. But not the film. Echoing its own difficulties with beginning, *Kind Hearts* now shows the same reluctance to close. There are so many ways in which a film could end, why choose one? So Hamer both chooses one, and doesn't choose; leaving things undecided, unclear.

Released from the guilty verdict, Louis leaves the prison to find jubilant crowds. And there both Sibella and Edith are waiting for him outside the gates. To which one should he show his love? Which one should he kill? Caught between possibilities (the fate of the flirt), Louis repeats to himself a couple of lines from Macheath's air from John Gay's *The Beggar's Opera* (1728), 'Have You Heard a Frolicsome Ditty':

> How happy could I be with either,
> Were t'other dear charmer away.

The next lines, which Louis does not quote, are:

> But while you thus teaze me together,
> To neither a word will I say …

The song proclaims its own inability to utter the word of choice, opting instead for the ambiguous confusion of silence. And Macheath is certainly a well-chosen double for Louis, being a character based on a joke that confuses a criminal with a gentleman.

And so the film ends by looking beyond its own ending. The reporter from *Tit-Bits* reminds Louis of his memoirs, and suddenly we realise that Louis has not escaped yet. The trap may yet claim him with its deadly justice! His memoirs will be found and read, his guilt discovered! Or not. It is, in narrative terms, completely up to you.

That openness is Hamer and Dighton's invention. In Horniman's novel, the memoirs are simply returned unread, and Louis settles down to a lifetime of unpunishable bliss, marred only by the faintest reverberations of guilt. And that makes perfect sense. After all, this is a film where manners are everything. And manners would dictate that a

Edith waits ...

Sibella waits ...

Louis hesitates ...

gentleman would never consider reading the private memoirs of an innocent (as he has just been proved to be) gentleman. Only a flaw in the manners that Louis abides by would secure his execution.

America refused the openness of Hamer's ending. Louis is the anti-Raskolnikov, the criminal who refuses to suffer. The American censors knew this, and, by their own lights, quite rightly insisted that he should then be made to suffer. It would surely weaken public morals to show that someone can commit murder and feel no guilt, that one might even flourish and live a more successful life as a result. In the American version, Louis gets caught.

Apparently, there were censorship problems in Britain too, and these either created the entirely apt openness of the ending, or nearly led to an American-style ending here (the anecdote isn't quite clear). Here Peter Tanner, the editor of the film, describes to journalist David Benedict the problems the film had with the British censors:

> In the original script, Louis got away with it. But the censor decreed that he must pay for his crimes so the end was rewritten before shooting began. We then had to submit the finished film. The censor John Trevelyan, Hamer and I had a very good lunch at The Ivy to discuss it. All through lunch Trevelyan refused to talk but had a sheet of paper with all the objections lying on the table. I'd worked on secret documentaries as part of my war service and had learnt to read upside down, so by the time we came to it, I'd read all his notes. We didn't get away with everything though.[56]

Hamer was no stranger to problems of censorship. He had to soften the coarseness of *It Always Rains on Sunday*, and to be particularly sensitive around the original novel's treatment of criminal guilt:

> Perhaps the most radical alterations, however, are those dictated, not by a director's whim or a script-writer's fancy, but by the exigencies of the British censorship. The author allows Whitey, literally, to get away with murder. By implication, also, Tommy is to be hanged for a crime he did not commit. Now this sort of thing is constructed by the jealous custodians of our moral code and the British way of life to be a slight on British justice: therefore it cannot happen. It is no good quoting police records. The Censor, too, is larger than life. Thus somewhere outside the range of the camera the Censor watches like a good angel over Tommy and remorselessly administers British justice.[57]

Perhaps Hamer resented this interference and actively tried to redress it, when making *Kind Hearts* only a year later.

Whatever happened around the debate on *Kind Hearts'* ending, it's clearly a lucky thing that the film ends, or refuses to end, so well. Before *Kind Hearts*, Hamer was the artist of trapped lives, an advocate for individuals caught in false and stultifying situations they cannot escape. The endings of *Dead of Night*, of *Pink String and Sealing Wax*, of *It Always Rains on Sunday*, all return the central characters to their traps; though now they are supposedly reconciled to them, ready to live out their lives within the circumference of their limitations. And this is quite unlike what happens at the end of *Kind Hearts*.

In this respect, critics have long made claims for Hamer's possible indebtedness in those earlier films to Marcel Carné, concentrating on the air of doom at the end of films like *Quai des brumes* (1938). And maybe it's just that the end of *Kind Hearts* subtly recalls the open-endedness of the French director's later film *Les Enfants du paradis* (1945), both in its melancholy evocation of the life of the actor, but also in the suspended inability to decide between two loved women.

In *The Cinema 1952*, Hamer talks of *Kind Hearts* as something that presented:

> the most agreeable possibilities. Did these possibilities generate intentions, or had previously latent intentions generated the possibilities? Looking back, I prefer to think the latter, though I remember no feeling at the time of being animated by stern endeavour, but merely the fact that it was fun to write, fun to argue about, fun above all to shoot.[58]

If in its making the film operated in the uncertain gap between possibilities and intentions, then that was always Louis's predicament too.

Louis ends by hesitating, still stuck between options of loving, of killing. Here possibility is a form of despair. And then, as he vacillates, Louis learns of his Freudian slip: that he has left his memoirs in the cell and risks being caught. You might wonder if Louis doesn't in fact long to be caught, if behind his desire for the endlessly open doesn't linger a greater need for judgment, punishment, even for his own death.

When some minutes before the end of the film, Louis's memoir ends, the film goes on to show us that his story is not just something contained within that memoir's elegant self-representation. Louis's life is more ragged, more human than that. Sibella's scheming had shown us that Louis's plotting is fallible; that there are more artists in the world than one. And now, the film's own scheming appears as another example of that, either as another irony or an instance of grace. Perhaps the film is telling us that it is Hamer and Dighton who are the ultimate contrivers of Louis's life, and not Louis himself. Or did Hamer want the last twist to reveal to us that life is bigger than those who make plots out of their lives? Louis is no longer in control.

The moment of the ending celebrates openness in another sense too. For it opens an escape door from the closed system of Louis's self-referential egotism. For Louis, addiction to the perpetually open is itself a form of imprisonment. Hence the symbol of his life-story literally remaining behind bars. But now the film suddenly escapes from this self-imprisonment into a larger world, a world of other stories, other selves. Kingsmill affirmed that it is not in the nature of things that the mysticism of evil should triumph in the end. The film quietly agrees, though not in the expected sense. It doesn't simply impose retribution on poor murderous Louis. At the end, the film tells us that Louis, living in possibility, in a world apparently unconstrained by the limitations of other people, is actually bounded in the nutshell of his own ego. And beyond that is the greater openness of life, something that is thankfully bigger than any of us.

Hamer declared that *Kind Hearts* 'extended the horizons of laughter'.[59] Having lived with this film for many years, and having worked so intensively on it for months, I feel that he was absolutely right. The fun that Hamer and the crew had making *Kind Hearts* really does communicate itself in the film. It dazzles, it entices, it flirts. It is in a peculiar way a joyful film. Though that joy lives both with and in spite of the strange constriction of Louis's personality. Perhaps my sense of Louis has made *Kind Hearts* seem too heavy and dark. Yet Louis's addiction to death, like the family vault where the D'Ascoynes watch over the living, truly is at the heart of this film. Yet for a film so bright, so sparkling, it would be wrong to end on such a note. The depths of the film – and it is as deep as any film made at that time, as deep as Carné, or Reed, or De Sica – are in the service of a comedy that looks beyond the confines of Louis's surface style. Ultimately *Kind Hearts* celebrates living, in its sardonic way, with an endless and always original vitality. There really is nothing else like it; unlike Louis, it has no double.

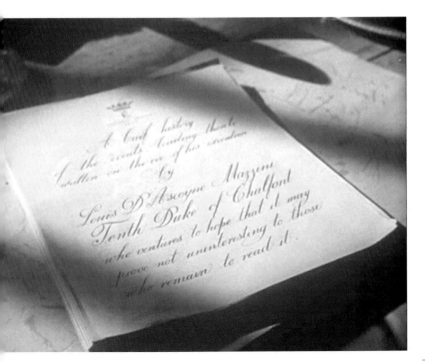

KIND HEARTS AND CORONFTS

NOTES

· ·

For publication details, see Bibliography.

1 William Shakespeare, *Macbeth*, IV, iii, 23–4.
2 Robert Hamer, 'Introduction to *Kind Hearts and Coronets*', in Roger Manvell and R. K. Neilson Baxter (eds), *The Cinema 1952*, pp. 52–3.
3 Although it is a commonplace of criticism around the movie that Balcon disliked *Kind Hearts* at the time of its release, it is difficult to find any proof of this, apart from later anecdotes and the fact that, by some accounts, Hamer had a hard time at Ealing. On the other hand, Leonard Mosley, in the *Daily Express* opening-night review (June 1949), reports that Balcon ('the most temperamental personality in British films') had declared the film to be 'the best of his comedies'. This is shortly after the release of *Passport to Pimlico* and *Whisky Galore!*.
4 Francis Koval, '*The Studio*: Sir Michael Balcon and Ealing', p. 8.
5 Ibid., p. 9.
6 Lindsay Anderson, *Making a Film*, p. 34.
7 John W. Collier, *A Film in the Making*, p. 52.
8 From John Ellis, 'Made in Ealing', p. 119.
9 Lindsay Anderson doubts the real influence of documentary on Ealing films: 'It was inevitable that British features should become more realistic as a result of the war, but whether as a result it is legitimate to associate them with the movement which started with *Drifters*, and during the war gave us many feature-influenced documentaries, is questionable' ('British Cinema: The Descending Spiral'), p. 6.
10 Evelyn Waugh, *The Diaries of Evelyn Waugh*, p. 783.
11 Koval, '*The Studio*', p. 8.
12 Quoted in Brian McFarlane (ed.), *Sixty Voices: Celebrities Recall the Golden Age of British Cinema*, p. 235.
13 Freda Bruce Lockhart, 'Interview with Hamer', p. 75.
14 Michael Balcon, '10 Years of British Films', p. 38.
15 Charles Barr, *Ealing Studios*, p. 119.

16 Quoted in McFarlane, *Sixty Voices*, p. 135.
17 Ibid., p. 61.
18 Ibid., pp. 57–8.
19 Alec Guinness, *Blessings in Disguise*, p. 199.
20 Lockhart, 'Interview with Hamer', p. 74.
21 Collier, *A Film in the Making*, p. 57.
22 Lockhart, 'Interview with Hamer', p. 75.
23 Michael Balcon, 'Film Comedy', p. 25.
24 Raymond Durgnat, *A Mirror for England: British Movies from Austerity to Affluence*, p. 116.
25 Andreas Missler, *Alec Guinness: Seine Filme – sein Leben*, p. 45. Translation by Dr Christopher Hamilton.
26 Lockhart, 'Interview with Hamer', p. 74.
27 E. F. Watling, *Kind Hearts and Coronets* and *The Castaways*, p. 9.
28 T. E. B. Clarke, *This Is Where I Came In*, p. 142.
29 Hugh Kingsmill, 'Introduction' to *Israel* [p. 37] *Rank*, p. vii.
30 Ibid., p. x.
31 *Sunday Dispatch*, 26 June 1949.
32 Quoted in McFarlane, *Sixty Voices*, p. 124.
33 Ibid., p. 235.
34 Quoted in Robin Cross, *The Big Book of British Films*, p. 89.
35 Quoted in McFarlane, *Sixty Voices*, p. 111.
36 Lockhart, 'Interview with Hamer', p. 74.
37 Durgnat, *A Mirror for England*, pp. 162–3.
38 Ibid., p. 51.
39 Collier, *A Film in the Making*, pp. 56–7.
40 James Laver, *Dandies*, p. 111.
41 Nik Cohn, *Today There Are No Gentlemen*, p. 23.
42 Quoted in Anthony Slide, *Fifty Classic British Films, 1932–1982: A Pictorial Record*, p. 73.
43 'Hamer, with his sense of loyalty, his capacity for friendship (though with a strictly limited number of people), his brilliant but mordant wit, engendered great affection in all who were allowed to know him well, but you had to know him well. He was, alas, subject to great emotional stresses and strains in his private life. At intermittent periods he was

unable to impose upon himself an essential discipline. Despite his early brilliant success, he rarely came to terms with himself, and it almost seemed that he was engaged on a process of self-destruction' (Michael Balcon, *Michael Balcon Presents ... A Lifetime in Films*, p. 163).

44 Kingsmill, 'Introduction' to *Israel Rank*, p. ix.

45 Gary O'Connor, *Alec Guinness the Unknown* (London: Sidgwick & Jackson, 2002), p. 271.

46 Catherine de la Roche, 'That "Feminine Angle"', p. 32.

47 Lindsay Anderson, 'Review of *Kind Hearts and Coronets*', p. 131.

48 John Ellis, 'Made in Ealing', p. 103.

49 Don Ottavio's aria, 'Il mio tesoro intanto/Andate a consolar,/E del bel ciglio il pianto/Cercate di asciugar./Ditele che I suoi torti/A vendicar io vado,/Che sol di stragi e morti/Nunzio vogl'io tornar.' 'On your affection relying,/I leave her to your care./Ease all her tears and sighing/And comfort her despair./Tell her I go to serve her,/Tell her that I shall avenge her!/To him who made her suffer,/Justice and death I bear!' From Wolfgang Amadeus Mozart and Lorenzo Da Ponte, *Don Giovanni*, trans. by Norman Platt and Laura Sarti.

50 G. Campbell Dixon, 'The Year's Work in the Feature Film', p. 27.

51 *The Times*, 27 June 1949.

52 Lockhart, 'Interview with Hamer', p. 74.

53 Robert Hamer, 'A Free Hand', p. 62.

54 D. A. Yerrill, 'The Technique of Realism', p. 24.

55 John Russell Taylor, 'Introduction' to [John Dighton and] Robert Hamer, *Kind Hearts and Coronets*, p. 6.

56 Quoted in David Benedict, 'Kind Hearts and Cold Killers', *Independent*, 5 May 1985. This anecdote is misremembered, since at the time of *Kind Hearts'* release, Sir Sidney Harris was President of the BBFC, and Arthur Watkins was Secretary. Trevelyan didn't join the BBFC, then as a part-time examiner, until 1951.

57 Collier, *A Film in the Making*, pp. 7–9, 10.

58 Hamer, 'Introduction to *Kind Hearts and Coronets*', p. 52.

59 Ibid., p. 53.

CREDITS

....

Kind Hearts and Coronets

United Kingdom
1949

Directed by
Robert Hamer
Produced by
Michael Balcon
Screenplay by
Robert Hamer
John Dighton
Based on a novel by
Roy Horniman
Director of Photography
Douglas Slocombe
Editor
Peter Tanner
Art Director
William Kellner

© Ealing Studios Limited
Production Companies
J. Arthur Rank presents
an Ealing Studios
production
Released through General
Film Distributors Limited
Associate Producer
Michael Relph
Production Supervisor
Hal Mason
Unit Production Manager
Leigh Aman
Assistant Director
Norman Priggen
2nd Assistant Director
David W. Orton
3rd Assistant Director
John Hewlett
Continuity
Phyllis Crocker
Assistant Continuity
Susan Carbutt
Camera Operator
Jeff Seaholme
Focus Puller
Paul Wilson
Clapper Loader
P. Pollock

Stills Supervisor
Jack Dooley
Stills
Bob Penn
Special Effects
Sydney Pearson
Geoffrey Dickinson
Assembly Cutter
Seth Holt
2nd Assistant Editors
Roy Baker
John Jympson
Assistant Art Director
Bert Davey
Draughtsmen
V. Shaw
Jack Shampan
Norman Dorme
G. Bryan-Brown
R. Hopkin
R. Thurgarland
Costume Designer
Anthony Mendleson
Wardrobe Master
Ben Foster
Wardrobe Mistress
Edith Crutchley
Make-up
Ernest Taylor
Harry Frampton
Hairstyles
Barbara Barnard
Pearl Gardner
Assistant Hairdresser
Daphne Martin
Music Played by
The Philharmonia
Orchestra
Conductor
Ernest Irving
Soundtrack
'Il mio tesoro intanto' from
Don Giovanni by Mozart
Sound Supervisor
Stephen Dalby
Recordist
John Mitchell
Boom Operator
A. Steadman

Assistant Boom
Pat Wheeler
Dubbing Editor
Gordon Stone
Publicity
Pat O'Connor
John Newnham

Cast
Dennis Price
Louis Mazzini / Louis's
father
Valerie Hobson
Edith D'Ascoyne
Joan Greenwood
Sibella Holland
Alec Guinness
Ethelred D'Ascoyne,
Duke of Chalfont
Lord Ascoyne D'Ascoyne,
the banker
Reverend Lord Henry
D'Ascoyne, the parson
General Lord Rufus
D'Ascoyne
Admiral Lord Horatio
D'Ascoyne
young Ascoyne D'Ascoyne
young Henry D'Ascoyne
Lady Agatha D'Ascoyne
Audrey Fildes
Mrs Mazzini, Mama
Miles Malleson
Mr Elliott, the hangman
Clive Morton
colonel, the prison governor
Cecil Ramage
crown counsel
John Penrose
Lionel Holland
Hugh Griffith
Lord High Steward
John Salew
Mr Perkins
Eric Messiter
Inspector Burgoyne
Lyn Evans
the farmer

Barbara Leake
Miss Waterman, the
schoolmistress
Peggy Ann Clifford
Maud Redpole
Anne Valery
the girl in the punt
Arthur Lowe
Tit-Bits reporter

[*uncredited*]
Laurence Naismith
1st warder
Maxwell Foster
Stanley Beard
warders
Jeremy Spenser
Louis as a child
David Preston
Lionel as a child
Carol White
Sibella as a child
Cavan Malone
Graham as a child
Ian Collins
Dr Hallward

Harold Young
captain
Molly Hamley-Clifford
Lady Redpole
Leslie Handford
Hoskins, gamekeeper
Gordon Phillott
clerk of parliament
Richard Wattis
Louis's counsel
Peter Gawthorne
Fletcher Lightfoot
peers
Anthony Adam

Black and White
9,529 feet

106 minutes

Credits compiled by
Markku Salmi,
BFI Filmographic Unit

BIBLIOGRAPHY

· ·

Amies, Hardy, *Still Here: An Autobiography*
(London: Weidenfeld & Nicolson, 1984).

Anderson, Lindsay, 'British Cinema: The
Descending Spiral', *Sequence* no. 7, Spring
1949, pp. 6–11.

——, 'Review of *Kind Hearts and Coronets*',
Sequence no. 9, Autumn 1949, pp. 130–1.

——, *Making a Film* (London: George Allen
& Unwin, 1952).

Armes, Roy, *A Critical History of the British
Cinema* (London: Secker & Warburg,
1978).

Baines, Barbara Burman, *Fashion Revivals from
the Elizabethan Age to the Present Day*
(London: B. T. Batsford, 1981).

Balcon, Michael, 'Cameramen are "Gunners"',
Kinematograph Weekly, 9 January 1941, p. 30.

——, "The British Film During the War', in
Roger Manvell (ed.), *The Penguin Film
Review 1* (London: Penguin, 1946), pp.
66–73.

——, 'Film Comedy', in Peter Noble (ed.),
British Film Yearbook 1949–50 (London:
Skelton Robinson, 1949), pp. 25–8.

——, *Film Production and Management*
(London: British Institute of Management,
1950).

——, '10 Years of British Films', *Films in 1951*,
supplement to *Sight and Sound*, July 1951,
pp. 23–38.

——, *Michael Balcon Presents ... A Lifetime in
Films* (London: Hutchinson, 1969).

Barr, Charles, *Ealing Studios* (1977; Berkeley:
University of California Press, 1998).

Baudelaire, Charles, *The Painter of Modern
Life and other Essays*, ed. and trans. by
Jonathan Mayne (1964; London: Phaidon
Press, 1995).

BFI collections of material on Michael Balcon,
Dennis Price, Joan Greenwood, Valerie
Hobson, Robert Hamer and *Kind Hearts and
Coronets*.

Breward, Christopher, *The Culture of Fashion:
A New History of Fashionable Dress*
(Manchester: Manchester University Press,
1995).

Carmichael, Ian, *Will the Real Ian Carmichael*
(London: Macmillan, 1979).

Clarke, T. E. B., *This Is Where I Came In*
(London: Michael Joseph, 1974).

Cohn, Nik, *Today There Are No Gentlemen*
(London: Weidenfeld & Nicolson, 1971).

Collier, John W., *A Film in the Making*
(London: World Film Publications, 1947).

Cranston, Maurice, 'The Pre-Fabricated
Daydream', in Roger Manvell (ed.), *The
Penguin Film Review 9* (London: Penguin,
1949), pp. 26–31.

Cross, Robin, *The Big Book of British Films*
(London: Sidgwick & Jackson, 1984).

Danischewsky, Monja, *White Russian – Red
Face* (London: Victor Gollancz, 1966).

—— (ed.), *Michael Balcon's 25 Years in Films*
(London: World Film Publications, 1947).

de la Roche, Catherine, 'That "Feminine
Angle"', in Roger Manvell (ed.), *The
Penguin Film Review 8* (London: Penguin,
1949), pp. 25–34.

[Dighton, John, and] Robert Hamer, *Kind
Hearts and Coronets* (rev. edn; London:
Lorrimer Publishing, 1984).

Dixon, G. Campbell, 'The Year's Work in the
Feature Film', in *The Year's Work in the
Film, 1949* (London: Published for the
British Council by Longmans, Green, 1949),
pp. 23–9.

Durgnat, Raymond, *A Mirror for England:
British Movies from Austerity to Affluence*
(London: Faber & Faber, 1970).

'Ealing on Location', *Sequence* no. 6, Winter
1948–9, pp. 30–1.

Edwards, Tim, *Men in the Mirror: Men's
Fashion, Masculinity and Consumer Society*
(London: Cassell, 1997).

Ellis, John, 'Made In Ealing', *Screen* vol. 16
no. 1, Spring 1975, pp. 78–127.

Ford, Boris (ed.), *The Cambridge Guide to the
Arts in Britain, Vol. 9: Since the Second World
War* (Cambridge: Cambridge University
Press, 1988).

Guinness, Alec, *Blessings in Disguise* (London:
Hamish Hamilton, 1985).

Hamer, Robert, 'Introduction to *Kind Hearts and Coronets*', in Roger Manvell and R. K. Neilson Baxter (eds), *The Cinema 1952*, pp. 52–3.

——, 'A Free Hand', in *Sight and Sound*, vol. 28 no. 2, 1959, pp. 61–2.

Hobson, Valerie, 'An Independent Speaks', in *Films in 1951*, supplement to *Sight and Sound*, July 1951, p. 22.

Horniman, Roy, *Israel Rank* (London: Chatto & Windus, 1907).

Hunter, Allan, *Alec Guinness on Screen* (Edinburgh: Polygon, 1982).

Kingsmill, Hugh, 'Introduction' to *Israel Rank* (London: Eyre & Spottiswoode, 1948), pp. vii–x.

Koval, Francis, '*The Studio*: Sir Michael Balcon and Ealing', in *Films in 1951*, supplement to *Sight and Sound*, July 1951, pp. 8–9, 58.

Laver, James, *Dandies* (London: Weidenfeld & Nicolson, 1968).

Leech, Clifford, 'Dialogue for Stage and Screen', in Roger Manvell (ed.), *The Penguin Film Review 6* (London: Penguin, 1948) pp. 97–103.

Lockhart, Freda Bruce, 'Interview with Hamer', *Sight and Sound* vol. 21 no. 2, October–December 1951, pp. 74–5.

McFarlane, Brian (ed.), *Sixty Voices: Celebrities Recall the Golden Age of British Cinema* (London: BFI Publishing, 1992).

Manvell, Roger, 'Monsieur Verdoux', in Roger Manvell (ed.), *The Penguin Film Review 7* (London: Penguin, 1948), pp. 77–82.

—— and R. K. Neilson Baxter (eds), *The Cinema 1952* (Harmondsworth: Penguin, 1952).

Mayer, J. P., *British Cinemas and Their Audiences: Sociological Studies* (London: Dennis Dobson, 1948).

Missler, Andreas, *Alec Guinness: Seine Filme – sein Leben* (Munich: Wilhlem Heyne Verlag, 1987).

Mozart, Wolfgang Amadeus and Lorenzo Da Ponte, *Don Giovanni*, trans. by Norman Platt and Laura Sarti, *Opera Guide 18: Don Giovanni* (London: John Calder, 1983).

Murphy, Robert, *Realism and Tinsel: Cinema and Society in Britain, 1939–1948* (London: Routledge, 1989).

Neilson Baxter, R. K, 'The Structure of the British Film Industry', in Roger Manvell (ed.), *The Penguin Film Review 7*, pp. 83–90.

O'Connor, Gary, *Alec Guinness the Unknown* (London: Sidgwick & Jackson, 2002).

Perry, George, *Forever Ealing* (London: Pavilion, 1981).

Raynor, Henry, 'Nothing to Laugh At', *Sight and Sound* vol. 19 no. 2, April 1950, pp. 68–73.

Richards, Jeffrey and Anthony Aldgate, *Best of British: Cinema and Society, 1930–1970* (Oxford: Basil Blackwell, 1983).

Roberts, William, *Prophet in Exile: Joseph Mazzini in England, 1837–1868* (New York: Peter Lang, 1989).

Sladen, Christopher, *The Conscription of Fashion: Utility Cloth, Clothing and Footwear, 1941–52* (Aldershot: Scolar Press, 1995).

Slide, Anthony, *Fifty Classic British Films 1932–1982: A Pictorial Record* (New York: Dover Publications, 1985).

Slocombe, Douglas, 'The Work of Gregg Toland', *Sequence* no. 8, Summer 1949, pp. 69–76.

Stanbrook, Alan, '*Kind Hearts and Coronets*' in [John Dighton and] Robert Hamer, *Kind Hearts and Coronets*, pp. 9–14. First published in *Films and Filming*, April 1964.

Steele-Perkins, Chris and Richard Smith, *The Teds* (London: Travelling Light, 1979).

Taylor, John Russell, 'Introduction' to [John Dighton and] Robert Hamer, *Kind Hearts and Coronets*, pp. 4–7.

——, *Alec Guinness: A Celebration* (1984; London: Pavilion, 2000).

Tennyson, Alfred, *The Poems of Tennyson*, ed. by Christopher Ricks, 3 vols (London: Longman, 1987).

Terry-Thomas with Terry Dunn, *Terry-Thomas Tells Tales* (London: Robson, 1990).

Vargas, A. L., 'British Films and Their Audience', in Roger Manvell (ed.), *The Penguin Film Review 8*, pp. 71–6.

Von Gunden, Kenneth, *Alec Guinness: The Films* (Jefferson, NC: McFarland, 1987).

Watling, E. F., *Kind Hearts and Coronets* and *The Castaways* (London: Thomas Nelson & Sons, 1937).

Watkins, A. T. L., 'Film Censorship in Britain', in Roger Manvell (ed.), *The Penguin Film Review 9*, pp. 61–6.

Watt, Harry, *Don't Look at the Camera* (London: Paul Elek, 1974).

Waugh, Evelyn, *The Diaries of Evelyn Waugh*, ed. by Michael Davie (London: Weidenfeld & Nicolson, 1976).

——, *The Essays, Articles and Reviews of Evelyn Waugh*, ed. by Donat Gallagher (London: Methuen, 1983).

Wilson, David (ed.), *Projecting Britain: Ealing Studios Film Posters* (London: BFI Publishing, 1982). Introduction by Bevis Hillier.

Wilson, Elizabeth and Lou Taylor, *Through the Looking Glass. A History of Dress from 1860 to the Present Day* (London: BBC Books, 1989).

Withers, Googie. 'Acting for Stage and Screen' in Roger Manvell (ed.), *The Penguin Film Review 4* (London: Penguin, 1947), pp. 36–40.

The Year's Work in the Film, 1949 (London: Published for the British Council by Longmans, Green, 1949).

The Year's Work in the Film, 1950 (London: Published for the British Council by Longmans, Green, 1950).

Yerrill, D. A., 'The Technique of Realism', *Sight and Sound*, vol. 17 no. 65, Spring 1948, pp. 23–4.

ALSO PUBLISHED

If you would like further information about future BFI Film Classics or about other books on film, media and popular culture from BFI Publishing, please write to:

BFI Film Classics
BFI Publishing
21 Stephen Street
London W1T 1LN